CW01512700

THE DNA OF ENGAGEMENT

THE DMA OF
ENGAGEMENT

THE DNA OF ENGAGEMENT

A story-based approach to building trust and influencing change

David Pullan & Sarah Jane McKechnie

First published in 2024 by Intellectual Perspective Press

Book Interior and E-book Design by Amit Dey
(amitdey2528@gmail.com)

To find out more about our authors and books visit:
www.intellectualperspective.com

You won't be able to attract and retain great people if they don't feel like they are part of the authorship of the strategy and of really critical issues. If you don't give people an opportunity to be engaged, they won't stay.[1]

Howard Schultz

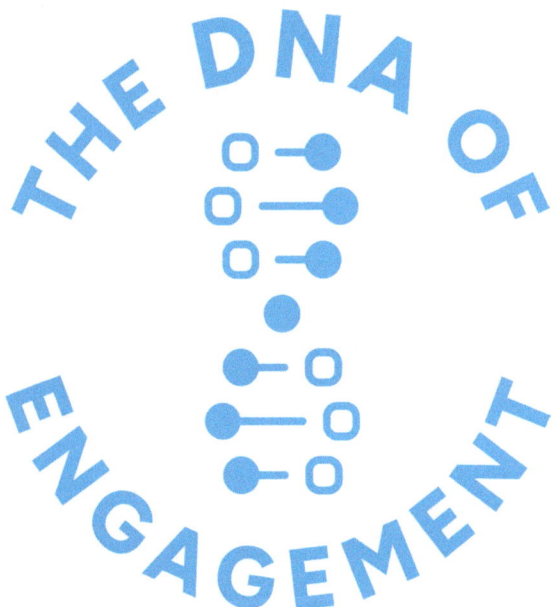

[1] Neff, Thomas & Citrin, James *Lessons from the Top, In Search of America's Best Business Leaders* (1999) Doubleday

TABLE OF CONTENTS

PRAISE FOR THE DNA OF ENGAGEMENT

This book is a great summary of everything David and Sarah Jane know about crafting compelling communications. Having tested out the DNA of Engagement with my teams at Aviva, I've seen the results it can deliver. Most of all it's a practical, thought provoking and enjoyable read. And short - a definite bonus for business books!

Dame Amanda Blanc – Group CEO Aviva Plc

I have used David and Sarah Jane's lessons in storytelling and leadership in the Navy SEAL Teams, a truly tough leadership environment where special men demand a special kind of leadership.

It is through the application of what you are about to read that I have been successful in the fast-pace and high-demands of that world. The DNA of Engagement is not another regurgitation of the same old leadership lessons. It is THE quintessential compass to guide your leadership approach and bring out the best in your people.

Follow this fresh and insightful prescription for building trusted engagement and your pursuit of inspiring others to change will become a reality. It works. Period.

**Jonathan Cleck, Tech Entrepreneur &
Navy SEAL Officer**

A wonderful book full of wisdom, humour and insight from cover to cover. Human interaction can be so easy when you know how.

Robert Dietrich – CEO Europe, Hiscox

As a manager I quoted David and Sarah Jane. As a leader I emulated them. And now, as a business founder, I advocate for them. You will too.

Lee Anderson –
Group Deputy CEO Specialist Risk Group

From treading the boards to teaching in boardrooms these two really know how to bring logic and emotion to the theatre of business.

Jeremy Connell- Waite -
Global Communication Designer IBM

'No one cares how much you know, until they know how much you care,' said Teddy Roosevelt. David and Sarah Jane have masterfully shown how to evidence that care. A delightful read.

Stephen O'Hearn – Chair of The Board of Directors,
Reinsurance Group of America, Incorporated

David and Sarah Jane are always full of energy, ideas and great advice. So is this book. Buy it and be delighted.

Simon Lancaster – Speechwriter and best-selling
author of CONNECT! How to inspire, influence and
energise anyone, anywhere, anytime.

As someone who's scaled two businesses I rely on logic, data and explanation. But this book opened my eyes to the power of storytelling when you want to scale at pace.

Michael Jones – CTO loveholidays
and formerly uSwitch.com

The DNA of Engagement reflects the tremendous substance that The Story Spotters bring to everything they do with us. It's a must read I will come back to time and again.

Enda McDonagh - Managing Partner PwC Ireland

Whenever I'm feeling stuck this book unlocks my thinking in an incredible way. It may well be the only communications approach that any businessperson will ever need. Genius!

Louise Bonham – CEO MAPP

Before this book even went to print my group had taken to using David and Sarah Jane's brilliant DNA formulation of Dream, Nightmare, Action!

Randy Olson - creator of the ABT Narrative Template and best-selling author of The Narrative Gym series

If you want to stand out at work, use the methods in this book. It's like being in the room with the voices, passion and expertise of David and Sarah Jane.

Chris Fenning – Award-winning author of The First Minute: How to start conversations that get results

David and Sarah-Jane bring such insight to the inner workings of the corporate environment. I believe that The DNA of Engagement will change the way businesses approach winning work and changing cultures.

Caroline Debenham – International Partner, Head of Sales Enablement, EMEA, Cushman & Wakefield

This is a gift from storytelling veterans that will weave its magic for you in and out of the boardroom.

Simone Heng, award-winning author of Let's Talk About Loneliness

THE FREE STUFF

This book comes with a free workbook that we've called the "Rehearsal Notes".

In it you will find three things.

- Space where you can reflect and plan your own application of the work.
- Links to videos that will give you a visual benchmark for some of the ideas.
- Some extra thoughts on how you can use The DNA of Engagement® "in the wild".

We chose to call them Rehearsal Notes because the pair of us spent many years as performers. If we took nothing else from that life, it was the knowledge that turning up on opening night without trying and testing our ideas during a rehearsal process is utter madness.[1]

We have no intention of turning you into a star of stage and screen. But we genuinely believe that you will gain a huge advantage if you put some strategic thought and practice into how you will show up at the moments that matter in your work life.

At the points where we recommend you use your Rehearsal Notes you will see this symbol.

Get all of the free stuff by signing up at www.TheDNAofEngagement.com

ENDNOTES

1. It's been years since either of us acted. But we still have nightmares about the possibility of standing naked in front of a West End audience having never seen the script.

WHY WE WROTE THIS BOOK

"This sh*t works!"

It's 1.15 on a drizzly November afternoon. Sarah Jane and I are drinking flat whites in a bare brick foyer that was once home to the UK's largest silk merchant.

At the tables around us people pick at the remains of their bento boxes and check their phones to see where their next meeting is.

This is Hoxton Square, the digital hub of Aviva, the British multinational insurance company.

Since February The Story Spotters® have been delivering The DNA of Engagement to leaders in every area of the business.

Our programme has one clear aim: make sure that those leaders leave with the tools to engage Aviva's 22,000 employees in the task of delivering Group CEO Dame Amanda Blanc's strategic vision.

For this to happen all of them will need to know how to have the collaborative conversations that will build trust and influence change.

And they will need to know how to do this consistently.

In fifteen minutes we will walk into the auditorium on level 4, plug our laptop into a screen that makes us feel like we're in an iMax franchise film, and start our final session.

If today's cohort follows the pattern of the previous nineteen, we'll hear laughter, we'll see focused energy, and we'll witness aha moments as people turn theory into practice.

A familiar face walks up to us.

"Hi, you two. I'm Brian. I was at your session on Tuesday. You see those people over there?"

Brian points to a group of six who are full of smiles as they walk out into the east London gloom.

"I've just spent two hours with them, and it could have been really tricky. But when I was preparing I put everything you spoke about into practice. And you know what? This sh*t works.[1] Why did nobody tell me about it twenty years ago?"

I look at Sarah Jane.

The beam on her face tells me that she is experiencing the same mental fist pump that is currently going on in my head.

Brian's right. This sh*t does indeed work.

Now ... STOP!

I want you to ask yourself one question.

"Am I reading the right book?"

If you are looking for tips on pure storytelling then the answer is no. You won't find any guidance on how to craft a personal success story, an origin story, or anything else with a hero, villain, beginning, middle and end in these pages. So please don't waste your money.[2]

But if you scream YES to these three statements then you're in the right place.

1. I need to find quick ways to turn resistance into agreement.

2. I need to have more collaborative conversations that guarantee action.

3. I need to know that what I say will be remembered and repeated.

Do I hear screams?

If it was you, then stay tuned. We're going to help you master some tried-and-tested story-based techniques that will help you achieve all of these things

But if you're still wondering, I want you to think about this.

Every day we all send ideas out into the world. Many of them are great ideas. And if those ideas develop and grow, we hope that they will start to make tangible differences to our work environments, our personal relationships and the world we all share.

- Innovative responses to changing market conditions will happen more quickly.

- Customers will become loyal advocates because they see and feel the steps being made to deliver an exceptional experience.

- Colleagues will rally behind strategic goals because they understand that what they are doing will benefit people, planet and profit.

But the sad truth is that too many of these ambitions either take too long to get off the ground or simply wither and die. And all because the great ideas behind them don't have the strength and structure to survive in a world that is becoming busier and noisier.

***The DNA of Engagement* is all about giving your ideas strength and structure.**

It's about building trusted relationships with colleagues and customers that encourage them to co-author the stories that will solve critical issues and drive strategic change.

We want to give you the tools to make sure that your ideas develop, grow, adapt, and reproduce in a world that is awash with content.[3]

Think of it as "survival of the fittest" for communication.

What's coming up?

I'm going to assume that you've read the Table of Contents, so there's no point in regurgitating that.

But for those of you who are intrigued by the tools you'll get on the journey ahead, here's a sneak peek at a few.

- The code that gets past the gatekeepers in the brain.
- The key to human understanding, planning and problem-solving.
- The three magic words that unlock engagement.
- A Nobel Prize winner's guide to storytelling.
- A sandwich millionaire's approach to digestible messaging.
- The art of making your numbers emotional.

Good aren't they?

But they will only become great when you put them into practice. And practice is at the heart of this book.

None of what we've written is designed to be skimmed passively and then left to gather dust. It is designed to be your coaching partner as you work on a relationship where you need to build trust, drive engagement and influence change.

If nothing "springs to mind" then later in the book we'll give examples of situations where we've seen The DNA of Engagement weave its magic.

The final option is that you could use the book as a retrospective to mull over a communication situation that you wish had gone better.

But whatever you do, please don't rush this. While the book may be short, you will get the most value from it if you put time aside for a bit of entelechy.[4]

Entelechy is the art of turning theoretical elegance into practical usefulness. How you choose to do that with The DNA of Engagement will of course be up to you.

You may be happy to pause every now and then and mull things over.

Or if you're a note taker and like to keep them all in one place, you'll definitely love the Rehearsal Notes we hope you've downloaded at www.theDNAofEngagement.com

But rest assured, whichever method you use, you are about to experience the exact process that The Story Spotters took Aviva's leaders through in 2023.

And now...meet Sarah Jane.

The Sarah Jane Adventures

Hello there. I'm Sarah Jane, the other founder of The Story Spotters.

I've called these bits The Sarah Jane Adventures because you're going to see me pop up with some additional thoughts as I travel across time and space in this book.[5]

Before we get started, I want to say a few words about leadership.

We developed The DNA of Engagement for leaders, but it's important to understand that we all have leadership responsibilities at every stage of our careers.

Some of you will be leading whole organisations. Some of you will be leading a business unit. Others will be leading a team, leading the thoughts in a meeting, leading clients to make a decision, or leading a new joiner on their first day.

Whatever leadership category you fall into you will be doing this. You will be holding the ladder up which others will climb.

The DNA of Engagement is about creating the conditions where others trust that you are holding the ladder steadily so that they have the confidence to climb. And you need them to climb, because without that your ideas will struggle to move forward in a sustainable way.

In February 2024 PwC Ireland released a survey saying that "44% of CEOs cite a lack of support from internal stakeholders as a significant hurdle for changing how their company creates, delivers and captures value."[6]

Basically, progress is possible, but progress is difficult if people don't genuinely buy in to making it a reality.

So, hold that ladder well and encourage others to climb.

This book will give you the skills to do exactly that by helping you build the trust and engagement that allows others to see your vision and want to deliver it.

And trust is where we are going to start.

We are going to look at Steven Spielberg's 1975 film *Jaws* because the central relationship between Chief of Police Martin Brody and Mayor Larry Vaughn is an object lesson in what happens when trust fails.

We'll discover three things.

1. Why trust is so central to engagement and sustainable change.

2. How easy it is to destroy that trust.

3. What you can do to make sure it doesn't happen to you.

ENDNOTES

1. Brian, one of your colleagues said this was a perfect example of your feedback style.

2. Of course we do that work at The Story Spotters. It's just not what The DNA of Engagement is about. Email us at hello@thestoryspotters.com if you'd like to know more.

3. Just like deoxyribonucleic acid (DNA) which is fundamental to our development, growth, adaptation and reproduction as living organisms.

4. There will be prizes handed out to those who can use entelechy in conversation.

5. If that reference means nothing then Google 'Doctor Who, Elizabeth Sladen.'

6. PwC Ireland Irish CEO Survey: embracing change in an age of continuous reinvention (Accessed February 2024) https://www.pwc.ie/reports/ceo-survey.html

ACT ONE

SCENE 1: WHY AND HOW TO BUILD TRUST

Jaws has trust issues

By any metric *Jaws* is a very successful movie. It won three Oscars and went on to spawn a franchise that has to date netted over $800mn at the box office. Not bad for an initial investment of $9mn.

But *Jaws* is also a perfect example of what happens to engagement and influence when trust fails. Let's just say that *Jaws* has trust issues.

For those of you who weren't traumatised in your teens here's a reminder of how the movie opens.[1]

It's the lead up to the Fourth of July weekend on Amity Island. Mayor Larry Vaughn is looking forward to a bumper start to the summer so that he can relieve the economic pressures that this small New England resort is facing.

But one morning, the remains of a young woman are found washed up on the shore.

The coroner concludes that it was a shark attack, and newly appointed police chief Martin Brody makes the unilateral decision to close the beach.

Vaughn isn't happy.

- He and Brody argue about the cause of death.
- The coroner is persuaded to reconsider his shark theory.
- The woman's death is put down as a boating accident.
- The beach is reopened.
- Four more people and a dog die.[2]
- Steven Spielberg makes a fortune.

As I said, great moviemaking, great storytelling and great business.

But terrible engagement and influence by Chief Brody.

And all because of a trust issue.

Three models for trust

Trust is essential if you want to drive engagement and influence change.

Stephen Covey calls trust "the glue of life ... the most essential ingredient in effective communication [and] the foundational principle that holds all relationships."[3]

Building trust needs a combination of emotional intelligence and strategic planning.

Neither of which Martin Brody displayed when he dealt with Larry Vaughn.

To understand what Brody got so badly wrong we're going to look at a formula.

In their book *The Trusted Advisor,* David Maister, Charles Green and Robert Galford developed **The Trust Equation**. It's a very powerful tool for understanding the elements that go into building trust.[4]

You can of course buy a copy of *The Trusted Advisor* if you want the full details. But if you want to cut to the chase, here's what you need to know.

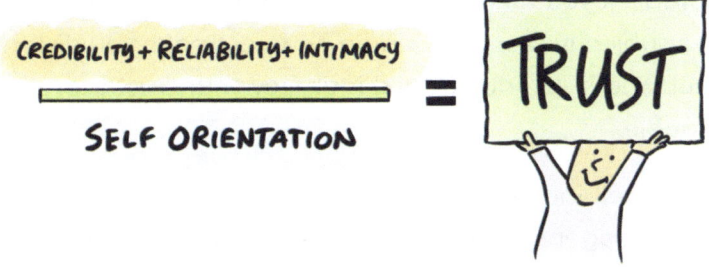

The first two elements on the top line are objectively measurable.

Credibility is about whether you are thought to be capable of doing your job. Your professional qualifications and resumé tick that box.

Reliability is about your track record of delivery. Again, your resumé, reputation and references tick that one.

Brody was doing just fine at this stage. He was a highly trained police officer. And he had a history of doing all the things that highly trained police officers do.

But it was the element of "intimacy" that started Brody's downfall.

Intimacy is the quality of being able to make people feel psychologically safe.

It's about empathy and understanding. It's about emotional intelligence. It's about creating an atmosphere of belonging and connection.

The score you get for intimacy might be empirically measurable if you take part in a 360° feedback exercise. But it is a subjective score based on how you make your listener feel. And if you don't build intimacy your trust score is in trouble.

Brody fell into this trap by failing to empathise with the mayor's agenda of keeping the beach open, and not showing that he understood Amity's need for a great opening weekend.

And when it came to the divisor of self-orientation things got even worse.

Self-orientation is all about whether you are perceived to be doing something to serve others and the greater good, or solely to serve your own needs. Again, it is subjective.

The mayor's perception of Brody was of someone who was throwing his weight around and demonstrating his own power.

The end result? An overall trust score that was much lower than it needed to be.

Now, you might notice that I've used the word "understanding" a few times. This is because ever since I read John Timperley's *Connective Selling*[5] I've been convinced that understanding is at the heart of intimacy and is therefore the bedrock of trust.

Timperley demonstrates this with his **Relationship Triangle.**

This wonderfully simple tool shows the six stages that all relationships go through. In fact you and I are going through them right now.

1. It starts with ACKNOWLEDGE. Basically, you acknowledge that I am a communications coach called David Pullan and I have written a book.

2. It then goes on to UNDERSTAND. This is where I want you to understand my ideas. And more importantly, I want to understand where you are coming from.

3. After that you will go into a period of reflection where I hope that you will ACCEPT that my ideas have some value.

4. Then, if you put the ideas into action and see the results, you might start to RESPECT them.

5. Continue doing this and we will eventually get to the stage where you will TRUST both me and my ideas.

The sixth stage, BOND, is relationship nirvana. It is where you wouldn't move without picking up the phone to me. But let's just agree that this is a summit that will most likely remain unscaled.[6]

What is important to note is that if I want to build trust then I need to keep seeking to "UNDERSTAND".

UNDERSTAND is the level where we get to feed the soil in which a strong relationship will bloom. It's where high intimacy and low self-orientation will do their best work.

Everything we've looked at here plays into one of the few pieces of neuroscience that I am going to throw your way, **Triune Brain Theory.**

In the 1960s Paul MacLean from Yale proposed that the brain is made up of three evolutionary layers.[7]

1. The Reptilian Brain that drives our survival instincts
2. The Limbic System that feeds our emotions and creates our memories
3. The Neocortex that deals with higher-order logical thinking

I'm sure that any of you who have studied psychology, or a related field, will point out that Triune Brain Theory has been widely debated and nuanced by advancements in areas like neuroimaging. It is now seen as a very simplified version of what actually takes place in our heads.

But one aspect of it remains relevant in contemporary neuroscience and holds a fundamental truth that is worth exploring.

Our logical ideas will only be accepted if they get past two gatekeepers in our listener's brain.

1. The first gatekeeper is instinctive. It is looking for patterns to determine safety. It is asking, "Can I trust you?"
2. The second gatekeeper is emotional. It will release hormones and drive emotional reactions in response to the question, "Do you understand me?"

Get past these two and you will gain access to the part of the brain that craves logic. It needs facts, loves data and wants to process a plan of how you will work together.

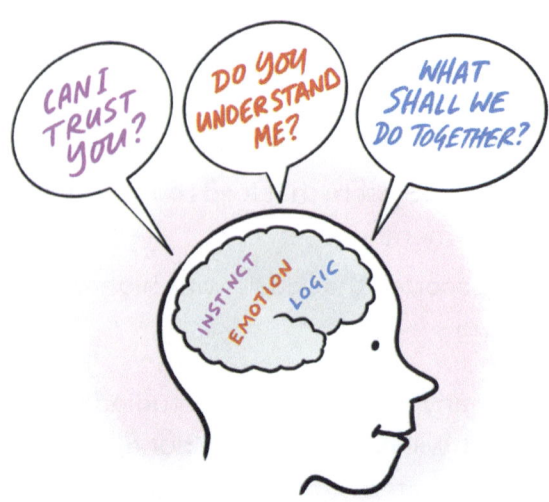

TRIUNE BRAIN

The big problem is that most of us head straight to the logical brain without dealing with the two gatekeepers who want safety and connection.

This, as we know, might lead to a 1970s shark-themed blockbuster. But it won't do you any favours in the trust, engagement and change game.

So, let's make sure that your ideas gain safe passage past instinct and emotion.

Let's get people leaning into the logic of your ideas and thinking, "I trust you because you understand me."

If you go to your Rehearsal Notes, we'll guide you through some ways to analyse where your levels of trust could be improved.

The Sarah Jane Adventures

Trust can be so hard to win and yet so easy to lose. It can sometimes feel like a rollercoaster ride.

One minute you think you are on a steady upward climb, and then all of a sudden something happens, and you go plummeting downwards.

So, if and when you experience that sinking feeling, it's the level of "Understand" that you need to work on.

Which is what we are going to look at now.

You're about to discover a pattern that is central to the way we have survived and thrived as a species.

In fact, because this pattern is so baked into our human experience, you can use it to get past the gatekeepers of instinct and emotion.

This, in turn, will build the trust that will drive the engagement and influence the change you are seeking.

We call this pattern The Other DNA of Life.

ENDNOTES

1. I read Peter Benchley's novel of Jaws during a beach holiday with my parents in South Australia. My father spent all summer fuming because I refused to dip even a toe in the water.

2. A certain British Prime Minister likened himself to the mayor of Amity during Covid. He's probably right ... but not in the way he intended.

3. Covey, Stephen R *The 7 Habits of Highly Effective People: Revised and Updated; 30th Anniversary Edition* (2020) Simon & Schuster UK

4. Maister, David H, Galford, Robert, Green, Charles *The Trusted Advisor* (2002) Simon & Schuster UK

5. Timperley, John *Connective Selling: The Secrets of Winning 'Big Ticket' Sales* (2004) Capstone

6. Sarah Jane's theory is that we only truly achieve 'bond' with our children. For me the jury's out even there.

7. Yale School of Medicine *A theory abandoned but still compelling* (Accessed January 2024)
    https://medicine.yale.edu/news/yale-medicine-magazine/article/a-theory-abandoned-but-still-compelling/

SCENE 2: THE OTHER DNA OF LIFE

The Other DNA of Life is a major factor in the way that we have developed, survived and thrived as a species.

It is so important to the human condition that if there was a Nobel Prize for Communication, The Story Spotters would claim that the role it has played has been as important as that of deoxyribonucleic acid.[1]

The Other DNA of Life underpins how we understand, plan and problem-solve during every waking moment of our lives.

This is how it works.

I want you to think back over your last week and remember something you absolutely had to do, or something you really wanted to do.

If you had achieved that thing without anything getting in the way what would that have meant to you?

For example, this weekend Sarah Jane and I invited friends over for Sunday lunch. I'd bought a beautiful piece of beef brisket that I wanted to slow roast following a Gordon Ramsay recipe.

I knew that if all went well, we'd spend a lovely afternoon around the kitchen table talking about the sort of non-sense that is usually heard at Chez Story Spotter outside of work hours.

That was my ideal world, my DREAM (D).

What was your dream?

Now we turn to the things that get in the way of the dream. It doesn't matter how small they are. It's anything that threatens your vision of an "ideal world".

For me it was the fact that my beef brisket bonanza was threatening to become a disaster because Mr Ramsay's recipe called for celery seeds. I'd made a slalom dash through the aisles of many supermarkets in the south-east of the UK, and I couldn't find them for love nor money.

That was my NIGHTMARE (N).

What was the "nightmare" that got in the way of your dream?

Now we think about what we can do to overcome that nightmare and get as close to our dream as possible?

In my case I asked Google to suggest substitutes for cel-ery seeds. Within milliseconds I discovered that the long-forgotten fennel seeds that were staring at me from the spice rack were the ideal alternative to throw into the slow cooker.

That was my ACTION (A). Lunch went just fine.[2]

What was the action that you took to get as close as you could to your dream?

Congratulations. You have just discovered The Other DNA of Life. The three narrative steps that underpin everything we do.

It's the equivalent of Act I, Act II, ACT III. Or Set Up, Conflict, Resolution.

1.   We set the objective of what we want.
2.   We analyse the obstacles.
3.   We make a plan.

Whether you are trying to cook the perfect lunch or trying to build an ideal world for the next generation, these are the steps we all take as sense-making, problem-solving animals.

Now, there are definitely other models out there that take a logical approach to setting objectives, analysing obstacles and making plans. Two that spring to mind are Barbara Minto's SCQA, and the military system called the OODA Loop.

SCQA (Situation, Complication, Question, Answer) is a powerful framework for structuring communication. It emphasises clarity, coherence and persuasive reasoning.

It starts by defining the Situation, then it identifies Complications, before formulating key Questions, and finally, providing Answers.

SCQA is the logical one.

OODA stands for Observe, Orient, Decide, and Act.

It's a rapid cycle iterative process that helps individuals and organisations adapt to changing situations by processing information, understanding context, making decisions, and executing actions faster than their opponents.

OODA is the ruthless one.

Both of these are great tools for making dispassionate, logical decisions.

But if you want to build trust, drive engagement and influence change you're going to need more than dispassionate logic.

You're going to need a deeply human element that is often overlooked in business communication: emotion.

Enter David Rock's SCARF model.

SCARF stands for Status, Certainty, Autonomy, Relatedness, and Fairness, and it puts emotion at the heart of human interaction.

It emphasises the important role that all of these areas play when you are trying to maximise supportive collaboration. Again, it is a very good model.

But wouldn't it be great if there was a communication model that combined both logic and emotion?

Well, there is. It's called The DNA of Engagement – a story-based approach to building trust and influencing change.

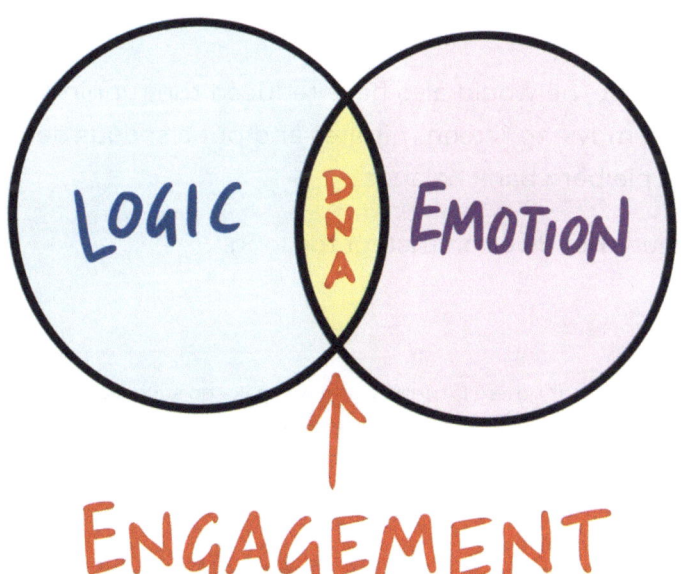

When we introduced our model to a group of strategy consultants I remember one of them saying that he loved how it combined the logical thought that he'd always been taught to use with the emotions that he'd always suspected were necessary.

From the next chapter onwards that's exactly what you are going to be doing.

You are going to discover how to take The Other DNA of Life and turn it into the logical and emotional DNA of Engagement.

You'll see how Martin Brody could have done the same thing in *Jaws* by taking Larry Vaughn's dreams and using them to build the trust and engagement that would have saved many lives.

Of course, he would also have reduced the running time of the movie to fifteen minutes and put a serious dent in the Spielberg bank balance.

But let's not dwell on that for too long.

ENDNOTES

1. Just for clarity, there is no prize and we make no such claim.
2. Here's the recipe if you're interested: https://www.youtube.com/watch?v=5n7-EZYaK-w

SCENE 3: THE DNA OF ENGAGEMENT

The need for narrative control

The terrible events in *Jaws* may not have happened if Martin Brody hadn't lost control of the narrative.

"Control of the narrative" might sound deeply untrustworthy to you as it has become intrinsically linked with the dark arts of "spin". There are connotations of mind manipulation and dominating others into a way of thinking.

At The Story Spotters all we mean by "control of the narrative" is the ability to actively shape how your listener interprets the subject you care about.

Think of it as setting a roadmap that engages people in the journey ahead and stops them from straying down any side alleys and dead ends.

To do this successfully you need to start with understanding.

If you go back to the Trust Equation, you will remember how important it is that you are understood to be doing something that serves other people or the greater good.

Now you may be thinking, "Well of course my idea serves others." But if there is even the slightest perception that this is not the case, your narrative control is in trouble.

Brody wanted to shut the beach because he wanted to save the people of Amity from a rogue shark. But because Mayor Vaughn was focused on creating a financially successful Fourth of July weekend for the town he couldn't see that.

His perception was of an ex-New York cop who didn't understand him at all and was throwing his weight around.

And it was this perceived lack of understanding that meant Brody immediately lost control of the narrative, and Amity was plunged into an avoidable chain of horrific events.

If only there had been a means by which Brody could have presented his argument so that he maintained narrative control, built trust, and engaged the mayor in a conversation that would have led to a better outcome.

Well reader, there is.[1]

How the DNA of Engagement controls the narrative

The DNA of Engagement controls the narrative by tapping into the DREAM, NIGHTMARE, ACTION sequence that we discovered in the Other DNA of Life.

It builds trust because its opening move is to connect to your listener's agenda and leave them in no doubt that everything you say is there to serve them.

It pulls people into your idea rather than pushing it on them.

Pushing is a terrible way to build engagement and influence change. If you push your idea onto someone, there is a good chance that they will push back. It's Newton's third law applied to human relationships.[2]

When Chief Brody opened by pushing his agenda to close the beach he created the conditions where Mayor Vaughn felt that he had to push back with his own agenda to keep the beach open. And this turned into a battle for narrative control where only the "loudest" voice would win.

This is a dynamic that is being played out every day in offices all around the world.

- Person A pushes for a budget of x to do y.
- Person B pushes back because they don't think y is even necessary.
- Person C joins in because they can't see how y could possibly cost x?
- And Person D doesn't care because their goal is all about delivering z.

It's like we've all decided to get involved in bare-knuckle boxing and can't understand why we constantly feel battered and bruised.

The DNA of Engagement avoids all this pain because it opens with understanding and focuses on collaboration.

The DNA of Engagement is a lover, not a fighter.

The DNA of Engagement 1.0

Let's get into start-up mode with your DNA of Engagement and find a minimum viable product.

To create the pull influence that will build trust and drive engagement you will need to follow three steps.

1. You will start by showing that you have understood the other person's DREAM.
2. Then you will keep them emotionally engaged by flagging up the NIGHTMARE that is getting in the way of their dream.
3. And finally, you will assure them that you have an ACTION that will help them achieve their dream.

These steps could be summed up as Connection, Conflict and Consequence.

For Brody it would have looked like this.

D. He would have connected by saying that he understood how important the Fourth of July weekend was to Amity's financial success and Vaughn's political ratings.

N. Then he would have introduced conflict by pointing out that both the success and ratings were under threat.

A. Before finishing with his plan which would have had the consequence of safeguarding the success and ratings.

This shift from pushing your own agenda to pulling someone in by focusing on their agenda is a tactic that I have seen work time and time again.

It worked for Brian who we met at the beginning of this book. And it worked for Georgina Smith.

George, as she is known, is Head of Wealth and Distribution at Liberty in South Africa. But in another life, she was one of the pioneer female rugby referees in the men's game.

One day, when we were on a Zoom call trying to stop our cats waving their bums at the camera, she told me this:[3]

> "David, it's hard enough trying to keep a bunch of hairy rugby players in check. But a female referee really has to be on top of her game. I always used to plan what I was going to say at key moments so I didn't lose control of the situation.
>
> I remember one match where the Guy's Hospital flanker landed a punch and knocked out the Gillingham fly half. It was a flashpoint and I knew that I had to keep a lid on it.
>
> I called over the Guy's captain and said, 'I know you want to win today **and** if you can do it in the spirit of the game then everyone will be happy. **But** right now that's not looking likely because your flanker's behaviour is unacceptable. **Therefore**, he's going to have to leave the field of play.'
>
> I planned it. I delivered it. And it worked."

Brilliant.

Go to your Rehearsal Notes where we'll help you build your own DNA 1.0.

The Sarah Jane Adventures

I love the story of George and the Fighting Flanker. And the best bit is that it had a very happy ending.

Reader, she married him. ♥

In reality there were many reasons why George's red card turned into a gold ring. But I'm sure that one of them was the way in which she controlled the situation by intentionally building a trusted narrative that was based on understanding the agenda of the Guy's captain.

We can often fail to do this when we are short of time.[4]

At moments of stress it's so easy to fall into the trap of rushing to a solution that is based solely on our own agenda.

Edward Brodkin and Ashley Pallathra, co-authors of *Missing Each Other: How to Cultivate Meaningful Connections,* wrote about the problems with this approach.

"While our culture encourages us to be assertive and push our own agenda, communication is often more effective when we start by meeting the other person where they are mentally and emotionally."[5]

So let's get straight into finding the way that you can do that.

If you look back at what George said to the Guy's captain on that wintry afternoon you will see that we have highlighted three words: "And, But, and Therefore."

In the next chapter you're going to use these words to turn your DNA 1.0 into a more engaging DNA 2.0.

ENDNOTES

1. Let's sing the next line together. 'It's called The DNA of Engagement.'
2. Every action has an equal and opposite reaction. And they say I didn't listen in physics.
3. We failed. Cats will be cats.
4. When aren't we?
5. Brodkin, Edward and Pallathra, Ashley *Missing Each Other: How to Cultivate Meaningful Connections* (2021) PublicAffairs

SCENE 4: THE WORDS THAT UNLOCK DNA 2.0

I promise you aren't about to get sucked into a whirlpool of three letter acronyms. But meet the ABT Framework.

The ABT Framework stands for "And" "But" "Therefore": three words that amplify the power of your initial DNA of Engagement.

I first came across the ABT Framework in May 2021 when I heard Dr Randy Olson being interviewed on a podcast.

Randy originally trained as an evolutionary biologist at Harvard and later became a documentary filmmaker at the USC film school.

As he spoke about his mission to help scientists make their work more understandable and more appreciated, I found myself doing something quite unusual. I slowed a podcast down from 1.25x to normal speed.[1]

For years I'd studied theories on logic and narrative structure. But Randy seemed to have boiled them down into a simple three-word formula.

That evening, I emailed him to say how I thought he'd discovered the missing link of story.

The following day he invited me and Sarah Jane to a Zoom call, which led to us joining some of his training sessions with various US government agencies.

During these sessions we met Park Howell, the host of the podcast *The Business of Story*, who often refers to Randy's framework as "the DNA of story".

But one night over a glass of wine Sarah Jane said, "I think it goes deeper than that. The logical problem-solving steps of 'And, But, Therefore' run right through us. They explain how we negotiate the story that we live every day. The ABT Framework is the other DNA of our lives."

Over the next couple of hours, we finished the bottle of wine, defined DNA as the DREAM, NIGHTMARE, ACTION sequence, and came up with the basis for The DNA of Engagement.

At about midnight I emailed Randy to tell him our thoughts.

This was his reply.

> ***The DNA is stunning.***
>
> ***I ran it by one of my most trusted colleagues.***
>
> ***He said, "Ooooooo".***
>
> ***I said, "We're done. I don't need anything further. You just said everything with that one sound."***

> *My recommendation is you throw EVERYTHING in your power behind THE DNA.*
>
> *I know a winning communications tool when I see one.*

So, thank you, Randy, for your seal of approval. In fact, thank you from all of us.

Without your trademark shoot-from-the-hip feedback everyone would now be reading a book called *The SPAR(Qu+E2) Approach*.

Well they wouldn't. It would have been terrible. But that's another story.

Let's get straight into seeing how we can use AND, BUT, and THEREFORE to turn your DNA 1.0 into DNA 2.0.[2]

The Dream weaver

Your first job in the DREAM section is to get your listener nodding in agreement.

You do this by showing that you have heard and understood the thing that is top of their mind, which is of course their dream.

After you've done that you use "AND" and the conditional clause "if ... then ..." to invite your listener to imagine a future where the realisation of their DREAM leads to a great outcome.

George did exactly this on that muddy rugby field.

She told the Guy's captain, "I know you want to win today <u>AND if</u> you can do that in the spirit of the game <u>then</u> everyone will be happy."

There was nothing in the opening part of the statement that the captain could disagree with. And in the second part she invited him to imagine a great outcome.

Yes, he wanted to win. And yes, like all rugby players, he wanted to have a few happy beers with the opposition afterwards knowing that he had won within the spirit of the game.

Uncontroversial. Full of understanding. And guaranteed to get nods of agreement.

Chief Brody could have done a similar thing with Mayor Vaughn.

He could have started with:

> "I know how often you've said that Amity is a summer town <u>AND if</u> we get the Fourth of July right <u>then</u> we guarantee our financial safety for the whole year."

Again, uncontroversial, full of understanding, and guaranteed to get the mayor nodding and imagining.

But Brody made the big mistake of starting with the nightmare of the shark.

Now, you might be thinking that this was absolutely the right thing to do. There was a monster out there and Brody had a duty to call it out.

But look what happened with that approach. Brody pushed, Vaughn pushed back, and people died.

Before we go any further, I want to highlight one situation where you should definitely start with the nightmare problem.

This is when you can guarantee 100% that everyone is in agreement about the nature, size and ownership of that nightmare. Then, and only then, should you start with the problem.

Without 100% agreement you will end up wasting time and money as people say, "Is it really a problem?" "How big is the problem?" "I don't think it's my problem."

That really is a nightmare.

In the vast majority of cases, you should start with the dream as it will quickly build trusted engagement and earn you the permission to talk about the nightmare.

The concept of permission-based argument is something I heard Barack Obama talk about on a podcast with his former director of speech writing Jon Favreau.

Favreau asked him how he would try to persuade the public today that there is a need to preserve democracy.

Obama said, "The starting point is to talk about the things uppermost on people's minds to give you a permission structure to get to democracy." [3]

I know I risk repeating myself, but always remember that the thing that is uppermost in people's minds is *their* dream, not yours.

Start by showing that you've heard that dream. Find common ground and build a strong bedrock of understanding that will allow you to bridge into the nightmare.

Let them know that you care.

In fact, to quote another ex-president of the USA, "Nobody cares how much you know until they know how much you care."[4]

The Sarah Jane Adventures

Since David is busy quoting US presidents and talking about push v pull influence, I am going to raise the game by combining the two.

We've said that the danger of push influence is that you run the risk of your listener pushing back. Well there is another danger that was summed up by the words of Dwight D. Eisenhower.

"Pull the string, and it will follow wherever you wish. Push it, and it will go nowhere."

So there you go. Push influence risks being met by either resistance or stasis. More reason to start with the DREAM.

But what do you do if you don't have an intimate knowledge of your listener's dreams? Or if you are facing a large group and there are lots of dreams?

Good questions. And this is exactly what the leaders at Aviva faced with their mixed teams across multiple locations.

The answer is to take the dream up a level and start with the agreed business objectives and what will happen if those objectives are achieved.

And if you are still lost then there's a further step you can take.

The UK speechwriter Simon Lancaster calls this step "arguing from morality."[5] It is essentially what George did when she talked about "playing within the spirit of the game."

No rugby captain was going to turn around and say, "Actually, George, I couldn't care less about the spirit of the game." Playing within the spirit of the game is the morally right thing to do.

Whichever option you choose, start by showing that you have understood and accepted the dreams of your listener.

In the words of the poet W.B. Yeats, "tread softly, because you tread on my dreams."

Go to your Rehearsal Notes and develop your DREAM section.

Welcome to the Nightmare

Congratulations. Your journey to trust has got off to a great start. You've engaged your listener by pulling them in and showing that you understand and care about their DREAM.

Now it's time to keep them engaged by introducing the conflict of the NIGHTMARE.[6]

This works so beautifully because the sudden turn from care and understanding into conflict comes as a massive surprise.

I know I promised that I wasn't going to bamboozle you with brain science but I'm going to make an exception here.

The power of surprise in storytelling lies in the fact that it triggers the release of a potent mix of cortisol and dopamine in your listener.

This cocktail sets off a mechanism of arousal and reward that makes them think, "OK. Things just got very real. What's going to happen next?"[7]

And the best way to mix this cocktail is by using the word "BUT."

People often say to us, "You shouldn't use 'BUT' because it wipes out everything you've said before." And we agree... but only to a point.

If you're giving feedback the last thing you want to say is,

"Well, you had a fantastic Q1. But then ... April happened!"

This is the classic compliment sandwich and definitely not the way to build trust and engagement.[8]

But we're not talking about feedback here. We're talking about powerful, strategic and intentional leadership communication that controls a narrative. And in this case the three letters of BUT do an enormous amount of heavy lifting.

- BUT throws on the handbrake and interrupts the expected direction of travel for your narrative.
- BUT changes the emotional tone from understanding connection to a disturbing warning.
- BUT plunges your listener into the depths of the NIGHTMARE.

And it does this because it says one of two things to your listener's emotional brain.

1. "Your dream isn't promised and you should really listen to what I'm about to say next."[9]
2. "Your dream is up a proverbial tree and something is going to have to change if you want to get it down in one piece."

BUT creates the conditions where people understand that change is necessary.

And change is the thing that we all want to influence. George did it perfectly.

After telling the Guy's captain that she understood his dream of winning, and that if he won within the spirit of the game then everyone would be happy, she said, "But right now that's not looking likely because your flanker's behaviour is unacceptable."

Suddenly his dream of sitting in the bar sharing a convivial beer had hit the nightmare of unacceptable behaviour. Something had to change.

We'll get to how you phrase that change in the next section. But before we do that I want you to notice three things.

1 "But" then "because"

George said, "<u>But</u> right now, that's not looking likely <u>because</u> your flanker's behaviour is unacceptable."

She started by referring to the captain's dream of winning in the spirit of the game, and then she said it was looking unlikely <u>because</u> of the fighting flanker.

She said WHAT was going to go wrong, and then WHY it was going to go wrong. The captain's agenda was still the star of the show.

Sticking to your listener's agenda in the NIGHTMARE section is crucial if you want to keep the engagement and narrative control that you started in the opening DREAM section.

2 The short "but"

Up to the word "because" George only said seven words: "But right now, that's not looking likely."

This is what Simon Lancaster calls a breathless sentence; a short, sharp shock designed to make people sit up and take notice. It interrupts the predicted pattern of the narrative dream with a nightmare.

See how punchy you can make your "but" statement.

3 Get in. Get out.

But leader, beware! Nobody wants to hang about in a nightmare. It's terrifying and sends all sorts of unpleasant chemicals running through our veins. We want to wake up.

Take a leaf out of George's book by getting in and out of the NIGHTMARE section quickly. It needs to be a metaphorical clip around the ear, not a lengthy period of holding someone's head down in a bucket of water.

We're aiming to disturb someone's thinking, not plunge them into terror.

The Sarah Jane Adventures

I hope you're getting into the swing of this now and noticing how the DNA mirrors the way we all operate on a daily basis.

We are constantly planning our lives and assessing the things that get in the way of those plans. It's such a natural process that half the time we're not even aware that we're doing it.

Let's quickly go back to *Jaws* and help Brody with his DNA of Engagement up to and including the Nightmare section.

It could go something like this.

"I know how often you've said that Amity is a sum-mer town AND if we get the Fourth of July right then we guarantee our financial safety for the whole year.

BUT that financial safety is in real danger because there is a shark out there that has killed once and doesn't look like stopping."

See how Brody is keeping the mayor's agenda of financial safety at the centre of his argument.

Like George, the "but" statement is a short sharp shock of what will go wrong. The explanation of why it will go wrong comes after the "because".

Why don't you have a go with your NIGHTMARE section?

A little more Action guaranteed

And now we've arrived at the payoff, your big idea. The ACTION.

This is where you will lay out your recommendation about how to overcome the Nightmare and get your listener's Dream back on track. And you've earned the right to do this because you've taken steps that are both emotionally and logically engaging.

Emotionally, you've followed a pattern that Jeremy Connell-Waite, the IBM Global Communications Designer, calls "excite-disturb-assure". [10]

- You've excited your listener by empathising with their dream.

- You've disturbed them by flagging up the nightmare that gets in the way of their dream.

- Now you are going to assure them, by showing the action that will get them back to their dream.

And logically you've stepped into the dialectic of Georg Wilhelm Friedrich Hegel, the nineteenth-century German philosopher.

- You've connected to your listener's thesis.

- You've put forward an antithesis.

- Now you are going to offer up your synthesis.

The trigger word for getting into the ACTION section is "Therefore". [11]

When George got to the ACTION she simply said, "Therefore, he's going to have to leave the field of play." And the Guy's flanker walked off for an early bath.

It was the logical next step, and the Guy's captain accepted it because George had first connected to his dream and then been clear about the nightmare.

Now you might be thinking that George was pretty free of emotion in her action section. And you'd be right. For the circumstances she found herself in, George did exactly what was needed to keep control.

But you're unlikely to face too many situations where you are sending rugby players off the pitch.

So, what do you need in your ACTION section?

Given that your emotional objective is to assure your listener that their dream is still attainable, you can afford to be more expansive with your sentence structure.

Longer sentences will counterbalance the emotions you've aroused with your short breathless sentence in the NIGHTMARE.

Let's go back to Chief Brody and see what he could have said.

His ACTION statement could have gone something like this.

> "THEREFORE, I want to work with you to guarantee our safety by closing the beach, taking the short-term hit, and paying the right person the right money to get rid of that thing once and for all."

There are a couple of things to note here.

1. Brody starts the ACTION section by saying *"THERE-FORE, I want to work <u>with you</u> to guarantee <u>our</u> safety."* By doing this he keeps the mayor's agenda of safety at the heart of his argument and uses the underlined words to turn it into a common interest.

2. Only then does he add the actions that will make that common interest a reality.

The concept of seeking common interest is a key negotiation technique in *Getting to Yes* by Roger Fisher and William Ury.[12] And it's one we suggest you adopt when using The DNA of Engagement.

By saying you want to work with someone, or "have a talk about our options" you are aligning yourself with your listener's Dream and inviting them to engage in a collaborative conversation that will co-author a solution.

This will lower your "self-orientation" number that we saw in the Trust Equation.

Have a go at adding some "common interest" to the ACTION of your DNA.

The Sarah Jane Adventures

Let's have a quick recap of what you've done so far.

- You've understood how trust works
- You've understood the need for narrative control
- You've understood the Other DNA of Life
- You've used this knowledge to build The DNA of Engagement 1.0
- You've used the ABT Framework to turn it into your 2.0

All of this has set a clear intention for your narrative.

In the next chapter you're going to turn your DNA of Engagement into something that is truly compelling.

You'll go from DNA 2.0 to DNA 3.0. And you'll do it by adding three elements that will really hit the head and the heart.

1. Narrative transportation
2. Emotional words
3. Numbers

ENDNOTES

1. If you haven't discovered this hack yet I thoroughly recommend it. Most podcasts are better with a bit of extra speed.
2. If you talk to Randy he'll say that his ABT Framework is all down to Matt Stone and Trey Parker from *South Park*.
3. Pod Save America Exclusive: Barack Obama talks Gaza, Israel and the 2024 election, 2023, https://www.youtube.com/watch?v=W7lgXXH_ v4 (Accessed January 2024)
4. Theodore Roosevelt for all you US president fans out there.
5. Lancaster, Simon *Connect: How to Inspire, Influence and Energise Anyone, Anywhere, Anytime* (2022) Heligo Books
6. Without a conflict there is no story. It's Act 2 of the three act structure.
7. Rodriguez, Giovanni. R. (2017) This is Your Brain on Storytelling: The Chemistry of Modern Communication (Accessed February 2024) https://www.forbes.com/sites/giovannirodriguez/2017/07/21/ this-is-your-brain-on-storytelling-the-chemistry-of-modern-communication/?sh=21631303c865
8. Other terminology is available.
9. Very useful when you are faced with someone who assumes they can get what they want through force of will alone.
10. Connell-Waite, Jeremy *Tell Better Stories* (2024) https://www.better-stories.org (Accessed February 2024)
11. This is true if you are an ABT purist. But in conversation you would be much more likely to use 'So'.
12. Fisher, Roger and Ury, William *Getting to Yes: Negotiating an agreement without giving in* (2012) Random House Business

SCENE 5: HOW TO TURN DNA 2.0 INTO DNA 3.0

Narrative transportation

It's early September 2021. Sarah Jane and I are sitting in the back row of an auditorium in the Museum of London waiting to present to Aviva's top 200 leaders.

Thanks to Covid this is the first time in eighteen months that many of them have been in the same room. The place is buzzing.

The clock ticks towards the hour and Amanda Blanc steps onto the central stage.

"Hello, all of you. I can't tell you how good it feels to be here with you today. We've all been through a terrible time in the last year and a half. Covid brought us closer to feelings of loneliness, fear and loss than any of us would wish. But I want to thank every single one of you. Because without you we wouldn't be in the place we are today."

> I think to myself, it's like she's talking to everyone as if they are the only person in the room.
>
> Sarah Jane leans towards me and whispers, "She's good, isn't she."

Let's just pause here.

As you read that, did you have a picture of that auditorium? Could you imagine the sound of the excited leaders? Did you see Sarah Jane leaning in and whispering to me?

If you answered yes to any of these questions you have just experienced narrative transportation.

Narrative transportation is the effect you get when you are so immersed in a story that you lose track of time and place. It's what happens to you when you are reading a great book.[1]

In an article on the role of narrative transportation in the persuasiveness of public narratives, Melanie Green and Timothy Brock say that its power lies in its ability to lower psychological barriers.[2]

Narrative transportation may not guarantee influence, but the way it brings together attention, images and feelings primes your listener's brain to want to know more.

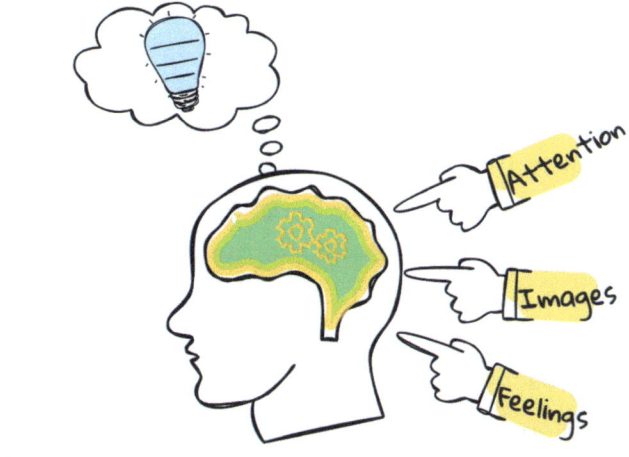

Narrative Transportation

So we're going to inject some narrative transportation into your DNA of Engagement.

The story I told you at the beginning of the chapter contains four elements that you can use to create narrative transportation in the DREAM section of your DNA of Engagement.

1. Time: As soon as you mention time it puts an anchor in your listener's mind and gives them something tangible to hang onto. I did it by saying, "It's early September 2021."

2. Place: When you add a place to the time you make the anchor more specific and therefore more solid. I did this by saying, "the back row of an auditorium in the Museum of London."

3. Character: Characters are the ultimate anchor point for our minds. They give us someone to identify with. So the sooner you add a character or two the better. And you get extra points for using a name because a name makes the character more real. You may never have met Amanda or Sarah Jane, but you can picture an Amanda or a Sarah Jane more easily than you can picture "a CEO" or "a coach".

4. Dialogue: All of us are fascinated by humans in action. Dialogue is a great way of showing this. It can be done in two ways.

   a. Outer dialogue: To quote *Hamilton*, the musical, outer dialogue puts you in the room where it happened. When you hear verbatim words you see humans in action with each other. I did this by quoting the direct speech of Amanda and Sarah Jane.

   b. Inner dialogue: Inner dialogue shows you in action with your thought process. It plays a big part in emotional engagement because it lets us into how you feel. I did this by saying, "I remember thinking, it's like she's talking to everyone as if they are the only person in the room."

Let's go back to Chief Brody in *Jaws* and see how he could have made his DREAM section more compelling by adding these four elements. He could have said something like this.

"I remember my first week in Amity. You called me into your office and said, 'Amity's a summer town AND if we get the Fourth of July right then we'll be good for the whole year.' I left that room thinking, if only every mayor focused on the safety of their town as much as they focus on their political future."

Sixty-one conversational words that contain,

- Time – First week in Amity.
- Place – Your office.
- Character – Brody and the Mayor.
- Dialogue – The mayor's words and Brody's thoughts when he left the room.

And those sixty-one words immediately engage the listener's mind. They act as a priming mechanism that makes them want to know more.

Have a go at putting some narrative transportation in your own DREAM section.

Emotion

Back in 2017 I worked with a wonderful leader by the name of Angela Brav. At the time, Angela was the European and North African CEO of the InterContinental Hotels Group.

As we were finishing a session one day she said to me, "You know, David, over the years I've come to a big realisation. As a leader, my main job is to read the temperature of the room and then change the temperature of the room."

It's a brilliant line that I've repeated to nearly every leader I've worked with since then.

Reading and changing the temperature of the room is all about reading and changing the emotional temperature.

It's about connecting to how people are feeling now and learning how to change that feeling. By doing so, you will keep them engaged with your subject and make them more likely to lean into the decisions you need them to make.

It's about making best use of strong emotions.

Jennifer Lerner, who holds the Thornton F. Bradshaw Professorship in Public Policy, Management and Decision Science at the Harvard Kennedy School, says that "strong emotions such as desire and fear are potent ... drivers of decision making."[3]

In your DREAM section you have already addressed desire by talking about what your listener wants to achieve and what it will mean for their future. Now you get to inject some fear in the NIGHTMARE section.

The word "BUT" starts this work by sharply putting the brakes on your empathetic connection.

"BUT" gives your argument a serious kick in the butt. It definitely changes the temperature in the room.

But we can go further by introducing two other elements.

1. Metaphor, and
2. Emotional words.

Metaphor

A metaphor is a powerful figure of speech that describes something by saying that it is equivalent to something else. It conjures up vivid imagery and connects directly to emotion.

Simon Lancaster says that the formula for metaphor is x = y. Music and poetry are full of these assertive connections.

- Love is the drug.
- Hope is the thing with feathers.
- Summer's a knife.

Because these assertions are crafted with such certainty they have a natural authority that leapfrogs rational thought and gets us nodding in agreement.

If we take the last example from *Cruel Summer* by Taylor Swift, her strong conviction that summer's a knife just gets us thinking, "Yes. Good point."

But if she'd said, "Summer's *like* a knife" she would have been using a slightly weaker form and only *invited* us to agree with her.[4]

This, of course, runs the risk that we disagree and say, "Hang on a second, Tay Tay. I'm not sure you're right. I think summer is more like a lazy wasp landing in my margarita."

So, let's stick to powerful metaphors and see how we can use them in the NIGHTMARE section to change the temperature in the room.

Given that your emotional intention in this section is to disturb your listener you need to find a disturbing metaphor.

To be honest you could stop reading this section right now and decide that you are always going to tell your listener that their goals are facing a NIGHTMARE. It would be a perfectly valid decision.

One of the reasons that Sarah Jane and I chose DREAM and NIGHTMARE for our process was because of their metaphorical power.

But I have a suspicion that you're more creative than that.

Instead of nightmare you could use car crash, nosedive, shitshow, cock-up … or anything else that feels appropriate and/or authentic to you.

But remember this.

1. **Use metaphors sparingly!** Yes, they are powerful tools. But that power can lead to them dominating a message and becoming a cliché. As the poet Clare Best told me, "Don't overdo the chilli." Which is of course a great metaphor in itself.

2. **Don't mix your metaphors!** Choose one and stick to it. Mixing metaphors is as pointless as mixing oil and water. You'll only confuse people if you "give them a recipe for success as they go to battle in a game of two halves."[5]

With these thoughts in mind, let's go back to Chief Brody and see if we can find him a single, clear and powerful metaphor that evokes the opposite of the mayor's dream of safety.

He could say:

"BUT that safety you want is <u>staring over the edge of a cliff</u>. Because everything says there's a shark out there that's already killed twice and doesn't look like stopping."

"Staring over the edge of a cliff." That doesn't sound very safe to me.

OK. You're probably thinking, "I'd never go that far in a business context." But why not?

Your aim in the NIGHTMARE section is to create a strong reaction that will keep attention and build engagement. And the best way to do that is by making the nightmare obstacle as vivid as possible.

I'm sure you can see that "staring over the edge of a cliff" would be a powerfully vivid metaphorical catalyst to create that reaction.

Dare yourself to choose powerful metaphors for your narrative statement. Be brave.

If you think you are going too far then you might just be approaching something very special. And you can always scale back later if you actually go too far.

As a theatre director once said to me, "Don't censor yourself in rehearsal. I need to see what you're capable of. Give me everything you've got, and we'll choose the best."

Emotional words

One big leadership question you have to ask yourself before you stand in front of anyone is, "Why is it me who is delivering this message?"

I would suggest that the only reasonable answer is because you can put your hand on your heart and say, "I have a strong opinion about my subject, and I need it to be heard now."

If you don't have an opinion and you don't need it to be heard, then you aren't really in the business of driving engagement and influencing change. You are merely imparting information.

And if that's the case then I recommend that you save yourself a lot of heartache by writing an email or a document that can easily be deleted or filed in the depths of a hard drive.

But that's not you. You're different. You're a change maker.

So how can you use emotional language to give your opinion and change the temperature in the room?

If we agree that your three emotional objectives in the DNA are to excite, disturb and assure, a good place to start is by taking your index finger, going to Google and finding synonyms for those words.

Just a quick search for "excited" gave me these.

- Delighted
- Thrilled
- Wired
- Fired up
- Impressed

Of course, those might not be the ones for you. But like using ChatGPT they are a starting point that can spark your own creativity.

Let's see what Brody could have done with his own DNA of Engagement.

"I remember my first week in Amity. You called me into your office and said, 'Amity's a summer town. AND if we get the Fourth of July right then we'll be good for the whole year.' **I left that room feeling really fired up**. It's not every mayor who focuses on the safety of their town more than they focus on their political future.

"BUT **I'm genuinely worried** that the safety you want is staring over the edge of a cliff because everything says there's a shark out there that's killed twice already and doesn't look like stopping.

"THEREFORE, **I want to work with you to guarantee our safety** by closing the beach, taking the short-term hit, and paying the right person the right money to get rid of that thing once and for all."

I want you to notice two things.

1. The phrases in bold, that suggest excite, disturb and assure.
2. The way that those phrases include the word "I" so that Brody takes ownership of his opinion.

Remember, your job goes beyond just delivering facts. Anyone can do that. Your job is to add your opinion to those facts.[6]

It's why you are in the room.

Think about what metaphors and emotional words you can use to make your opinion clear.

Numbers

I hope you are starting to discover ways that you can enhance your DNA of Engagement by adding some emotion.

But we can't leave it there.

Emotion may well be a vital driver of engagement and decision-making but you can't rely on it to do all the work if you want to get your ideas over the line.

Dave Trott, the award-winning advertising creative director, says that if you solely rely on emotion and don't add some facts it suggests that you have nothing to say about your product that you are proud of. Emotion alone is patronising and "consumers aren't dopes – they can spot that."[7]

What is true for products is equally true for important ideas. And the "consumers" you will be talking to are definitely not dopes.

Yes, they still have feelings, but they are rational and technical beings who need hard evidence if they are going to fully trust you and be influenced to change their thoughts and behaviour.

When I was working with Tina Higgins from Axa UK on a presentation about the future of claims she told me that her husband always says this.

"A person without data is just a person with an opinion."

I completely agree with this. A heartfelt opinion is great but it isn't enough when big budgets are involved.

So, let's look at how you can introduce some numbers that will add to your argument and build the trust and engagement that you are looking for.

Over many years of coaching teams on global tenders Sarah Jane and I have noticed that audiences are generally doing a mental cost/benefit analysis on up to five areas.

We call them the TIRES.

1. Time.
2. Income.
3. Risk.
4. Expense.
5. Stress.

For your message to tick the logic box you need to do some due diligence and kick the numbers on your TIRES.[8]

Here's how they work.

T.I.R.E.S	COST	BENEFIT
TIME	Wasting time.	Saving Time
INCOME	Leaving money on the table.	Making more money.
RISKS	Increasing or overlooking risk.	Minimising risk.
EXPENSE	Watching costs spiral.	Cutting costs.
STRESS	Sleepless nights.	Sleeping like a baby.

I'm sure you will recognise many, if not all, of these elements in the problems you get involved with on a daily basis.

When Chief Brody was crafting his DNA of Engagement, he could have considered the beneficial TIRES he was kicking for Mayor Vaughn.

- Time – helping Amity to reopen quickly.
- Income – making sure that Amity's long-term financial future was secure.
- Risk – stopping the shark from becoming a PR disaster.
- Expense – saving money by paying once for the right solution.
- Stress – minimising the panic that was sweeping the town.

It would have been overkill to use all of these TIRES. But any of them would have gone right to the emotional heart of Mayor Vaughn's DREAM of safety.

When you are looking for the TIRES you can use in your DNA you will have to make two decisions.

1. **What are the best numbers you can use?**
2. **Will you use them to illustrate a pain (cost) or highlight a gain (benefit)?**[9]

I'm going to suggest that you illustrate pain before you highlight gain.

In 1979 Daniel Kahneman and his associate Amos Tversky published a research paper that said people are more motivated by the fear of pain than they are by the promise of gain.[10]

In plain terms, the majority of us will react more strongly to the possibility of losing all the money in our pockets than to the possibility of doubling that money on the roulette table. This means that you should first look to kick the cost TIRES in your NIGHTMARE section.

Let's imagine that Chief Brody decides that his two most powerful cost TIRES are the risk of Amity staying closed for a long time and the income that the town will lose.

He could say this.

> "BUT I'm genuinely worried that the safety you want is staring over the edge of a cliff. Because everything says there's a PR disaster out there that will keep us closed for many summers to come (risk), and wipe at least $10mn from Amity's revenue (income)."

The twenty-six words after "because" hammer home Brody's point with a big dose of rational and painful data.

If you wanted to, you could now add some benefit TIRES to your ACTION section.

But you might not want to bother because they will probably emerge in the conversation that ensues. The whole point of The DNA of Engagement is to create the conditions for collaborative conversation and discovery.

However, you should definitely think about those numbers and prepare for the moment when people say, "Let's talk more about this."

Have a go at adding some compelling numbers to your DNA.

The Sarah Jane Adventures

This is the last time we're going to meet Chief Brody and Mayor Vaughn.

Before we say goodbye and wish them a happy shark-free Fourth of July weekend let's put all of Brody's DNA of Engagement together using narrative transportation, metaphor, emotional words and numbers.

It could go something like this.

"Larry, I remember my first week in Amity. You called me to your office and said, 'Amity's a summer town, and if we get the Fourth of July right then we'll be good for the whole year.' I left that room thinking, 'If only every mayor focused on their town's safety as much as they focus on their political future.'

"But I'm genuinely worried that the safety you want is staring over the edge of a cliff. Because everything says there's a PR disaster out there that could keep us closed for many summers to come and wipe at least $10mn from Amity's revenue.

"Therefore, I want to work with you to guarantee our safety by closing the beach, taking the short-term hit, and paying the right person the right money to get rid of that thing once and for all."

I don't know about you, but those feel like 141 words that could be delivered in just under a minute and would stand a pretty good chance of getting the mayor to engage and say, "Let's talk more about what we're facing here."

In the second part of the book we're going to look at how you can take a story-based approach to driving that conversation.

You'll learn:

- How to tell the stories that will support your DNA of Engagement.
- How to get others to engage more deeply by telling their own stories.
- How to create the space and time to build deeper trust.

All of which will add to the chances that you will influence the changes that need to be made.

But now, I think you've earned yourself a cup of tea.

 **INTERMISSION**

Tea? More like champagne. You've done some amazing work.

I want you to know one thing. If you put this book down now and do nothing except perfect the skills you've learned so far you'll be way ahead of the pack.

The vast majority of people won't even touch you when it comes to building trust, driving engagement and influencing change.

By creating your own DNA of Engagement 1.0 and turning it into 3.0 you've given your message an architectural structure that will protect it from falling down.

Architecture; that's a very good metaphor.[11]

Dave Trott, who I mentioned earlier, says that you will discover the secret of influence if you create an architecture for your argument that "encourages [your listener] in a certain direction" but allows them the freedom to contribute.[12]

Is that manipulative? Possibly, if it lands in the wrong hands.

But for you it means that you now have a framework for powerful and collaborative communication.

There is a wonderful TED Talk by Itay Talgam called *Lead Like the Great Conductors*. In it he highlights the benefits of contribution and collaboration by comparing the stories of two famous baton wielders.[13]

The first story is about Ricardo Muti who was the conductor at Milan's eighteenth-century opera house La Scala.

In March 2005 a meeting attended by nearly 800 workers, including all of the musicians who played under him, led to a resolution saying, "You're a great conductor. We don't want to work with you. Please resign."

People could see Muti's talent, but they were fed up with his need to control. Everything he did made them feel as if they were merely instruments of his vision rather than partners helping to create the orchestral story as a whole.

Talgam then compares Muti to the German-born Austrian Carlos Kleiber.

Kleiber was no stranger to control. But his control was all about guiding the journey from the first bar to the final note while creating the conditions where his musicians had the autonomy to interpret that journey.

When you watch Talgam's TED Talk you will see that Kleiber is almost dancing with delight at the contributions of the soloists. You will see the joy of the orchestra as their "stories" are heard within the structure of the whole piece.

It is collaboration and partnership in action.

This is what we are aiming for with The DNA of Engagement. A clear structure that gives you the confidence that you can control the narrative, combined with the ability to tell stories and hear stories that will bring that narrative to life.

And to get it right you're going to have to become a master of space and time.

Space and time were a key focus for Charlotte Otter as she completed her highly acclaimed MSc in Change Leadership at HEC Paris and Saïd Business School, University of Oxford.

All of her research led her to conclude that these two elements created the necessary conditions for those seeking to build trust.

Space was all about creating physical proximity and psychological closeness. And time was about clearing your calendar so you could be fully present.

So, I'm glad you're still here and that you haven't put the book down. Because from now on we're going to be looking at how you can make the best use of space and time to co-create the stories that will support your DNA of Engagement.

You're about to take trust and engagement to a whole other level.

ENDNOTES

1. Our son used to call it 'the story feeling' when we read to him at bedtime.
2. Green, Malanie and Brock, Timothy 'Understanding Media Enjoyment: The Role of Transportation into Narrative Worlds *Communication Theory Volume 14, Issue 4* (2006) https://academic.oup.com/ct/article-abstract/14/4/311/4110790?redirectedFrom=PDF (Accessed January 2024)
3. Lerner, J.S., Li, Y., Valdesolo, P., Kassam, K.S. (2015). Emotion and decision making. Annual Review of Psychology, 66:33.1-33.25.
4. This is called a simile if you ever need to know for a pub quiz.
5. Did you see what I did there?
6. This more than anything else will future proof you against the bots.
7. Trott, Dave *Campaign Asia* 'A view from Dave Trott; When logic is emotion' (Accessed March 2024) https://www.campaignasia.com/article/a-view-from-dave-trott-when-logic-is-emotion/485643
8. Years ago I heard about a similar acronym called RITES. If you own the rights to RITES then let me know and I'll buy you a beer as a thank you for the inspiration.
9. This probably doesn't need saying, but never ever make up a number. Nothing will kill trust quicker than numerical BS.

10. Kahneman, D & Tversky, A, (1979) Prospect Theory: An Analysis of Decision Under Risk. *Econometrica 47 (2)* 263–291 (Accessed January 2024) https://www.jstor.org/stable/1914185?origin=crossref

11. They're everywhere I tell you.

12. Trott, Dave, *One + One = Three*, 2015, Pan Macmillan

13. Talgam, Itay, Lead Like the Great Conductors, 2009 (Accessed February 2024)
https://www.ted.com/talks/itay_talgam_lead_like_the_great_conductors

ACT TWO

SCENE 1: WHY STORIES MATTER

I have a confession to make.

If you and I meet for anything other than a drink and a catch up, I'll probably have spent some time planning the stories I want to tell you.

- Positive stories about things I've heard about you.
- Disturbing stories about what I've seen other people in your industry going through.
- Reassuring stories about how they've overcome the challenges they face.

More importantly, I'll have thought about the questions I want to ask that will get you telling me some of your own stories.

Depending on your point of view this might seem:

A. Really creepy and verging on the manipulative, or
B. Really clever and strategically astute.

As you're still here I'm going to assume you went for B.

Peter Guber, the producer of films such as *Batman*, *The Color Purple*, *Midnight Express* and *Rain Man* once said that purposeful storytelling isn't show business, it's good business.[1]

I'd go one step further and say that it's purposeful story *co-creation* that is good business.

When I ask to hear some of your stories and tell you some of my own, I have one single goal: I want both of us to start "same paging".

"Same paging" is the process of creating a clear shared vision of the DREAMS, the NIGHTMARES, and the ACTIONS.

If you are looking for ways to improve your Customer Experience (CX) and Employee Experience (EX) then inviting these stakeholders to "same page" by co-creating the story is a vital skill.

This may feel like a long and winding road to travel if you are a fellow time-poor control enthusiast.[2]

But travel it we shall, because ultimately it will save you time, decrease the risk that problems aren't identified, minimise stress at an individual and a team level, and stop you wasting a lot of money.

Henry Daubeney, who was Global Head of ESG and IFRS Reporting at PwC and is now a much sought after non-executive director, has an interesting way of describing the problem that sits behind a lack of "same paging".

He says that the biggest challenge in most projects is that everybody speaks the same words but very few speak the same language.

We all hear the same things, but we all interpret the story differently.

Let's see how easy it is to fall into the trap of misinterpretation.

Read the following sentence and tell me what you think is going on.

> I don't know if you noticed but Jack's car was parked outside Diane's house again last night.

What did you come up with?

Are Jack and Diane having an affair? Is Diane's place a safe house that Jack uses for his sideline in harbouring defecting foreign nationals? Does Jack have very bad luck with the parking outside his own apartment?

To be honest your answer doesn't matter.

What matters is that your brain has just done something remarkable. It has instantly taken on board the following seven pieces of information.

1. There is a Jack.
2. There is a Diane.
3. Jack has a car.
4. Diane has a house.
5. It is night-time.
6. There is a repeated action.
7. Somebody is talking about all of these things.

And in a flash, your brain has interpreted that information by giving it a context, a motivation and a meaning. Your brain has created a story.

But, sadly, that story is probably not the one that I wanted you to create.

The truth is that Diane lives near the airport and poor old Jack has had to park outside her place for the third time this month because he has to catch a 7 a.m. flight to go and see his sick mother.

So, what went wrong?

Three things.

1. I had an idea.
2. I dumped all of the facts about that idea on you.
3. I assumed that you would arrange those facts into the same order that is in my head.

But you didn't. You came up with your own interpretation, your own story. And this is the "same words/different language" problem that Henry Daubeney talks about. It's a sorry state of affairs and it kills engagement and destroys trust on a daily basis.

So, what can we do?

Well, the good news is that you've already done a lot of the groundwork by designing the architecture of your DNA of Engagement. Now it's time for the interior decorators to come in and bring that DNA to life.

They will do this by spotting and sharing stories that will leave everyone with an accurate, vivid and repeatable vision of the dreams, the nightmares and the actions.

According to Kendall Haven (the only storyteller to take part in the DARPA programme to research the neural and cognitive science of how stories exert influence) vivid accuracy is a vital element of success.[3]

"Stories only have one metric that really matters: Does your material lodge accurately and vividly into the minds and memories of your intended audience so that they will readily recall them to affect their attitudes, beliefs, values, and behaviour?"[4]

Let's make sure your material does exactly that.

ENDNOTES

1. Speaking of *Midnight Express*, when you meet Sarah Jane, ask her about the time when she and a US Marine had drinks in an Istanbul café. Truly hair raising.
2. 'Control enthusiast' is a much nicer description than control freak, don't you think?
3. The Defense Advanced Research Projects Agency (DARPA) is a research and development agency of the United States Department of Defense that is responsible for the development of emerging technologies in the military.
4. Haven, Kendall. *Story Smart* 2014 Libraries Unlimited

SCENE 2: HOW TO TELL YOUR STORIES

Two types of story

Generally speaking, the stories that you will tell to support The DNA of Engagement will fall into one of two categories.

1. Closed loop stories
   a. These are the stories that have a defined beginning, middle and end. They follow a complete DNA pattern of Set up, Complication, Resolution. In their grandest form they can often follow what Joseph Campbell called "The Hero's Journey". Think of the *Star Wars* films, *Harry Potter* and yes ... *Jaws*.

2. Open loop stories
   a. These are the stories with a cliff-hanger ending that get you wondering, "What happens next?" They follow a partial DNA pattern and often end with a nightmare. Think of any episodic television series that you have binged. *Breaking Bad*, *Ozark*, *Game of Thrones*.

In The DNA of Engagement open loop stories will be your best friend.

When you learn to craft and tell these types of stories you will make your listener want to fill in the missing gaps and demand to continue the conversation. That's a real measure of engagement.

So how can we generate these golden moments?

Robert Shiller, the Sterling Professor of Economics at Yale, may have the answer.

In 2013 Shiller was awarded the Nobel Memorial Prize in Economic Sciences for his book *Narrative Economics* in which he examined the qualities that have helped certain ideas achieve viral status.[1]

According to Shiller these ideas capture the collective imagination because they fulfil the following four criteria.

1. Vivid – They are more colourful than any competing stories.
2. Varied – They come from many sources.
3. Simple – They are easy to digest.
4. Told often – They are shouted from the rooftops at every opportunity.

All of these elements are relatively simple to master when you understand the skills and commit to practising them consistently.

I'm about to give you the skills. The rest is up to you.

Make them vivid

As a species we are endlessly fascinated by human interaction.

I've heard it said that we spend about seventy percent of our time talking about who did what to whom, where they did it, when it happened, and what the outcome was.

I don't know if scientists have discovered a gossip gene, but I bet there is a very good evolutionary reason why we behave like this. It's probably because vivid stories allow our brains to make the patterns that help us decide what to do, what to avoid, and how to avoid it.

If we want to make those stories vivid and fire up the neurons in our listener's brain, then all we need to do is call on our four friends of narrative transportation.

1.   Time – when did it happen?
2.   Place – where did it happen?
3.   Character – who did it happen to?
4.   Dialogue – what did they say or think?

A good rule of thumb to follow is this.

If you can't draw it, don't say it.

PIZZA   PROCESS

Any vague term is the death knell of vivid communication.

And yes, I'm talking about "core competencies", "feedback loops", and my personal bugbear ... "added value".

In your Rehearsal Notes you'll find links to some videos called *The Ezy-Street Stories*. These are some examples we've created to give you a benchmark of what a vivid story could look like. You'll also see a storytelling score-card. We recommend that you record your own stories on your phone and mark yourself against the areas we have suggested.

The vivid story muscle is one you can develop if you commit to consistent practice.

Make them varied

If you only have one proof story, particularly around your NIGHTMARE section, then people will start to ask questions.

- "Is this really a problem that needs solving now?"
- "Could it just be a random outlier?"
- "If it's only happened once then don't you think it might just go away?"

To avoid this, you need to find a varied selection of stories to prove your point.

One of the biggest complaints I get from clients is that they don't have any stories to tell.

My answer is that we all have plenty of stories to tell. We just don't notice them.

So, what can you do?

You can take a leaf out of the playbook of one of the most popular television series of all time.

In the decade between 1994 and 2004 *Friends* dominated the airwaves around the world.

If you go to Wikipedia and search for *List of Friends Episodes* you will see that 231 out of the 236 titles start with the words, "The One with/where..." The other five use "after," "in," "at," or "without."

In my opinion it is utter genius. How many times have you been in a situation where someone has said something like, "Have I told you about the time when...?"

So, to find your varied stories you are going to play *Friends*.

In the Rehearsal Notes you'll find "The Friends Story Log". It will help you start a daily practice of noting every relevant story that demonstrates the DREAM, NIGHTMARE or ACTION around your idea.

You'll give each story a *Friends*-like title, such as

- The One Where Beccy Told Me She Wished She Had Better Data or
- The One When Barry Bored the Board

To these you will add some prompts using the narrative transport elements. Before you know it you will have a varied bank of relevant stories.

And look at it this way; if nothing else works, you might end up with a hit TV series on your hands.

Keep them simple

For many people the fear of disagreement stops them from truly stepping up and taking powerful ownership of their story.

But there is a danger that is even greater than contradiction. You might get ignored.

I'm going to let you into a secret.

We all have lazy brains. And every day our lazy brains are bombarded with information. Unless your information is simple to digest your listener's lazy brain will say, "Hang on a second. This is taking a hell of a lot of energy to untangle. I'm going to spend my glucose somewhere else."

So how can we make our information simple?

Let me introduce you to the PRET structure.

The PRET structure

Like any aspiring actor, I spent a lot of time not acting. On those non-acting days, I would often work as a chef and butler for directors' lunches in the City.

One Monday I was working with Fiona, a fellow chef who I'd known for a year or two.

"Morning, Fiona. Good weekend?"

"Not bad. A bit tiring. My husband's friend Julian is staying with us and he's got some crazy idea about a sandwich shop."

Julian's sandwich shop went on to become Pret a Manger and in 2018 he sold the Pret group for £1.5 billion.

One simple idea with one big return.

Now, as I'm sure you know, Pret a Manger means ready to eat. Well we're going to make your message ready to understand.

We'll guarantee you get the best return by turning your explanation into inspiration and making it simple to digest.

Meet the PRET structure.[2]

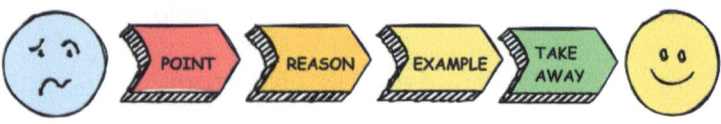

Let's imagine you are part of a risk team, and you want to illustrate the NIGHTMARE of people not adopting a new IT system, before bridging into the ACTION that will overcome that.

1. POINT

    Nobody in business is going to listen to you unless they know that you have a clear point to make. And that point needs to be short and sharp like a good headline.

    It can be as simple as saying, ***"We need to inspire our teams to use the new procurement system."***

2. REASON

    After your point you need to back it up with a reason or motive.

    Motive is a key element to building empathy and identification, and it is central to engagement.

    Now, for better or worse, big numbers are very motivating. In fact, when I am working with teams that are pitching for investment I recommend that they don't say too many sentences without adding a big number.

Therefore, I suggest that you add some of your TIRES numbers in the "reason" section.

"We need to inspire our teams to use the new procurement system **because they're still falling back on manual processes that are costing us nearly €1mn a quarter."**

3. EXAMPLE

And now comes the part where you get to illustrate your point with a quick example.

"We need to inspire our teams to use the new procurement system because they're still falling back on manual processes that are costing us nearly €1mn a quarter.

"I was in Paris with Monique last Tuesday and she said she felt like she was banging her head against a brick wall. She spends hours making the logical case for change but none of that is translating into action."

Notice the four elements of narrative transportation.

1.   Place – Paris

2.   Character – Monique

3.   Time – Last Tuesday

4.   Dialogue – She said she felt like she was banging her head against a brick wall.

Powerfully engaging details, as we've established.

But never fall into the trap of adding irrelevant details.

You don't want to say, "I was in Paris with Monique last Tuesday. The smell of freshly baked baguettes wafted up from the street below and she said she felt like she was banging her head against a brick wall. She spends hours making the logical case for change but none of that is translating into action."

Weird, isn't it? Unless those freshly baked baguettes are material to the slow adoption of the procurement system.

With any example you need enough detail to make your meaning vividly clear. But not so much detail that people suddenly think they are at an Open Mic Spoken Word Competition and the theme is French bread sticks.

Vivid examples aren't difficult to achieve. But they must obey the American author Elmore Leonard's tenth law: leave out the parts that people want to skip.[3]

5. TAKEAWAY

After your example you need to finish with your key takeaway or call to action. Don't leave anybody in any doubt about what you want them to think or do as a result of what you've said.

"We need to inspire our teams to use the new procurement system because they're still falling back on manual processes that are costing us nearly €1mn a quarter.

I was in Paris with Monique last Tuesday and she said she felt like she was banging her head against a brick wall. She spends hours making the logical case for change but none of that is translating into action.

So I think that Ruth should create a team to gather some powerful stories from our offices. Stories that will show how the system is simple to use and how it frees up people to do the work they really want to focus on."

During lockdown Neil Bearden who, at the time, was Professor of Decision Sciences at INSEAD, asked me to support him with his online MBA and EMBA story courses.

One of his many quotable lines was that if people don't have a clear point to take away from your story you can end up looking like a drunk who is stumbling down the road with a key in your hand but no lock to put it in.

The PRET Structure has you covered. Twice! You start with your point and you end with your takeaway.

Look for the PRET worksheet in your Rehearsal Notes.

Rehearsal notes

Tell them often

There is simply no point in having a great idea with great supporting stories if you don't have a strategic plan to get out there and tell them.

I like to see stories as logs that you throw on the fire of engagement and influence.

You need to throw enough of them to make sure that the conversation keeps blazing, but not so many that you smother it.

Here are six questions that will help you come up with your strategy.

---

1. Who do I need to talk to?

2. What do I need to say?

3. Where does this need to happen?

4. When is the optimum time to make it happen?

5. Why am I saying what I am saying?

6. How do I need to do it? (Face to face, online, 1–1, team meeting, conversation, presentation etc.)

You'll find a Story Strategy planning worksheet in your Rehearsal Notes.

The Sarah Jane Adventures

Me again. Did you miss me?

All the steps we've taken you through might seem a bit daunting. But they will soon become second nature if you tackle them one by one and put them into practice every day. It really is about consistency, reflection and refinement.

In a moment we're going to look at possibly the most important story skill of all; how you can get other people to tell their own story.

But before we do that I want to say a few words about how you can bridge into telling your own story.

The first thing to note is that you must never start by saying, "I want to tell you a story." It might have worked as a catchphrase for the old British comedian Max Bygraves but no seven words in the English language are more likely to set off BS alarms in a boardroom.

"For example" on the other hand is the perfect bridge into a story.

This simple couplet will prime your listener's brain for all the benefits of story without mentioning the s-word once.

The sooner you get to "for example" the better.

Another thing to add to your practice list.

But now let's get stuck into getting stories from other people.

ENDNOTES

1. Shiller, Robert J. *Narrative Economics* (2019) Princeton University Press
2. Yes, I know there's a PREP model out there. But you don't get a sandwich story with that.
3. Leonard, Elmore 'Writers on Writing' 2001 (Accessed April 2024) https://www.nytimes.com/2001/07/16/arts/writers-writing-easy-adverbs-exclamation-points-especially-hooptedoodle.html

SCENE 3: HOW TO GET STORIES FROM OTHERS

I can't imagine the day when I don't look forward to hearing other people's stories. Story spotting has given me much more than our company name.

I've discovered small family restaurants that only a local would know about and I've salvaged relationships that looked like they were dead in the water.

I remember a networking event in the 1990s where I was introduced to a very imposing master of the financial services universe as, "David, an actor who helps people speak better."

"Ah," said the master. "It must be very intimidating to be around all these smart city types when you're just an actor."

I decided to take a leaf out of Abraham Lincoln's playbook by thinking, "I don't like this man. I must get to know him better."

"Well, I seem to be getting away with it so far," I said. "But listen. I've been told you've got a yacht in the Scilly Isles. I've never been. If I was going to spend the perfect week there, what should I do?"

An hour later we'd shared the best part of a bottle of red wine, I'd learned which pint to order at The Mermaid in Hugh Town, and we'd swapped business cards. A week later we met for coffee to talk about the people in his network who might be interested in what I do.

Getting stories out of others really is the superhighway to their hearts.

You can feel the warmth rising, the ice melting, and the trust building as you give people the space to engage in a pastime that not many provide. So how do you do it?

Well, the simple answer is that it's a bit like learning to walk as a baby. If you really want to do it then the skills will follow.

But there are definitely some things that you can put into practice that will multiply the chances of you hearing some stories that will build trust, drive engagement and influence change.

How do you ask for a story?

The short answer is you don't.

One of Sarah Jane's best friends had a surprise birthday lunch recently and we were all asked to think of an activity we could do during the meal to bring the whole table together.

I suggested that each of us could put an everyday object in a bag that we could then pass around. We'd take turns to pick something out and see if it triggered a story.

Well, you've never seen a WhatsApp group blow up so quickly.

"It's alright for you. Story is your job."

"I can never think of any stories?"

"I hate performing."

I quickly took a back seat and let my suggestion slide.

Then on the day of the lunch I decided to talk about the first time I'd met the birthday girl. Suddenly a veritable bushfire of tales swept around the table.

You see, the word "story" might have people scampering for the hills in a cold sweat. But if you create the conditions for storytelling people can't help themselves.

How to create the conditions for storytelling

Given that storytelling can make some people feel very vulnerable we need to create a space where story can happen naturally.

The good news is that it's not too difficult if you follow these steps.

Tell a story to get a story

As you can see from the birthday lunch example, the best thing you can do if you want to get a story from other people is to tell one of your own.

If you want to hear more stories about the DREAMS, NIGHTMARES or ACTIONS that will lead to change then start by giving examples and insight from your own experience.

- Where have you seen moments of greatness that need to be replicated?
- Where have you seen people tripping up on the road to greatness?
- Where can you imagine things being done differently to benefit all?

You'll be collecting all these stories in your *"Friends* Story Log". And once you have told your story people will have a subconscious awareness that they are in a SaaS environment (Story as a Service).

Ask for the story you want

There are three types of stories that are going to be very powerful for you to unearth as you look to build engagement.

1. Experiential stories
2. Emotional stories
3. Aspirational stories

Experiential stories

Experiential stories are about the actions that took place. Who did what with whom? Where did it happen? When did it happen?

They give you a clear picture of a situation. And that clear picture helps you avoid the "Hazy Hollow" where everyone thinks they are on the same page, but they can't put their hand on their heart and swear it is true.

A great way to trigger an experiential story is to use a technique I learned from the American storytelling expert Matthew Dicks.[1]

Matthew looks for what he calls "First, Last, Best, Worst" stories.

For example, if you are trying to get someone to open up about the problems that they see getting in the way of change in the NIGHTMARE section, you might ask them one of these questions.

- What happened the <u>first</u> time you noticed this going on?
- Where were you when you <u>last</u> noticed this behaviour?
- What is the <u>best</u> example you remember of this going on?
- How have you seen this playing out at its <u>worst</u>?

I'm sure you can think of many ways to phrase some first, last, best, worst questions.

Emotional stories

There is an old saying in the story world that a good story helps you *see* what is going on, but a great story makes you *feel* what is going on.

Emotional stories go a step further than experiential stories by drilling into the feelings that were generated by what happened, or the feelings that could arise in the future.

I wouldn't recommend asking for an emotional story as your opening gambit because you will be asking people to step into potentially vulnerable areas. They will be revealing their subjective inner landscape rather than an empirically true outer landscape.

But asking "How did x make you feel" is a very powerful follow-up after you have established the experiential story.

A safe way to get to an emotional story is to offer a range of options rather than just one.

If you say, "That sounds as if it was a very worrying situation for you," you risk hearing "Yes it was" or "No it wasn't".

But if you ask, "Was that a worrying situation, or did you see it as more of a challenge," they might land on one of those options.

Or even better, they will pause in contemplation, search their memory banks, and then come back with a third option that is much richer than anything you could have imagined.

A key thing to remember when dealing with emotional stories is that you have to create a space where it feels safe for the other person to open up. So don't rush this process.

Give people a gift by setting aside the time for their experience to be witnessed.

Aspirational stories

Aspirational stories are a wander into the future. They are a great way to get people imagining how things might work out perfectly if their DREAM comes true.

Many years ago, I supported a team that had twenty-seven site visits around the world as part of their bid for a large global contract. Every one of those visits was an opportunity to understand the DREAM scenario that the client aspired to.

At an early account planning meeting I suggested they take a MoSCoW approach to these meetings.

MoSCoW is a prioritisation tool that I believe started in the world of software development.

It stands for,

- Must Have
- Should Have
- Could Have
- Won't Have

I said, "What would happen if you developed a board with the MosCoW quadrants? You could pre-populate them with things that other clients have said they must have, should have, could have, won't have in similar projects? Then you could tell stories about what that looked like and ask the client to tell their own stories. Finally, you could get the client to reposition the ideas in a quadrant that feels right to them."

They went with my suggestion, and surprise surprise, at every site visit stories were flying around the room. My client said they could feel the trust and engagement building there and then.

Unsurprisingly they won the bid.

Helping someone to define their aspirational future is a gift to both you and them.

The gift to you is that they have told you what great will look like, so all you have to do is work out how to get them there.

But the gift to them is that you have helped them clarify their dream, which in my experience can often be a bit high level and theoretical in many business scenarios.

There's another sort of aspirational question that the son of a friend of ours has used to great effect in many job interviews.[2]

If the interviewer asks him if he has any questions, he says this.

"I do, actually. Let's imagine it's six months in the future and you've given me the job. What would I have done that would make you turn to the CEO and say that I was the right person to hire?"

On one or two occasions he's just had the job spec read back to him. But generally, people have paused and said, "Great question."

They've then gone on to paint a vivid picture of their dream, which our friend's son has used to help build his case.

A perfect example of aspirational story spotting as a tool for engagement and influence.

Peeling the onion

A lot of experts suggest that a good way to get stories out of people is by saying, "Tell me about a time when..."

Sarah Jane is not a fan of this approach.[3]

Of course, you should definitely expect that question in a strengths-based job interview. And you would be mad if you didn't think of some powerful stories to use as answers.

But if you ask that question in general conversation, it runs the risk of sounding like a command. And commands put people on the spot. This can make them clam up.

A much better approach is to ask a question that starts with "When" "Where", or "Who."

These words will get a reply that involves time, place or character; the key triggers for a story.

- When did you first notice this going on?
- Where were you when it happened?
- Who was there?

All you have to do then is keep adding these questions to help the other person uncover the layers and get to the heart of their story. You peel the onion.

While you are doing this you might find moments when a little voice in your head says, "Ooo, that's interesting. I wish they'd tell me more about that."

This is when you can use the "conversational right click".

The "conversational right click" has the same function as a right click in computing: it helps you reveal more context.

It's a simple three step process.

1. You wait for the other person to take a tiny pause.
2. You tell them that what they've just said is interesting.
3. And then you add, "Can you tell me more about that?"

In all our years of coaching and consultancy we've never had someone reply, "No. I won't." People love talking about themselves when they know that the person in front of them is fully present and is genuinely interested.

Another great way to peel the onion is by using what I call "Wouldy Questions."

I told you about our friend's son and his killer aspirational question. He got the other person to imagine the positive future and then said, "What would I have done that would make you turn to the CEO and say that I was the right person to hire?"

He could just as easily have asked, "How would you and the CEO know that you made the right decision by bringing me on board?"

The key to a "Wouldy Question" is to use "how" or "what" then follow it with "would" to get your listener to unlock their imagination.

Unlocking the imagination is a vital skill to master if you want to drive engagement.

It gets people creating their own image of a successful dream. And that self-created image has a special power that Sarah Jane and I discovered when we studied cognitive behavioural hypnotherapy.

At a very high level there are two schools of hypnotherapy: direct and indirect.

If you were a smoker and you came to me for help, I might choose to take a direct approach.

This is where I would tell you that the next time you go to the pub and a friend offers you a cigarette you will be amazed at how easy you find it to say no.

The danger is that the next time you go to the pub and you end up taking a cigarette you are left thinking, "David is a terrible hypnotherapist."

However, with an indirect approach I might say, "I wonder how you would feel when you find the strength to say no?" Or "I wonder what you might do that would make it easy for you to say no?"

I would be asking you a "Wouldy Question".

As soon as I did this I would notice your eyes flick away briefly as you start to build a picture of your dream and the actions you will take to overcome any nightmares.[4]

That eye flick is the moment when you are unlocking your imagination and creating your own story.

And the special power in that moment is that if you create your own story of success you are much less likely to prove yourself wrong than if someone like me imposes a story on you.

So if you are serious about driving engagement and influencing change, start to peel the onion by asking "Wouldy Questions" and helping people to imagine their own story.

Lean in

The Human Givens Institute[5] is an organisation that raises awareness of the fundamental physical and psychological needs we must meet if we want to live a mentally healthy and fulfilled life. They call these needs the Human Givens.

Their belief is that by meeting these givens, we will improve "all forms of human endeavour and interaction."

Some of the emotional givens are:

- Security – a safe environment which allows us to develop.
- Attention – giving and receiving it.
- Emotional intimacy – the feeling that someone accepts us "warts and all."

Leaning in during a conversation sends a powerful signal to the other person that these needs are being met. And when I say "leaning in" I mean physically leaning in.

The Canada based British body language expert Mark Bowden has a wonderful mental image to help you do this.[6]

When you are in a conversation imagine that you are standing or sitting under a door frame.

You have three choices you can make about where you position yourself in relation to the door frame.

1. You can lean back and be behind the door frame which risks looking disengaged or deeply disinterested.

2. You can be right under the door frame as if it was running directly down the middle of your body. This is a good neutral position.

3. Or you can lean in. Get the door frame just behind your ears and see how much it improves your presence and how much it makes the other person feel that you are there for them.

In your Rehearsal Notes you'll find a link to The Door Frame video where I demonstrate Mark's concept for you.

Show you've been changed

When we are with our friends there is no better feeling than knowing that what we have said has had a good reaction.

We love it when our story of facing a huge challenge is met with open mouthed shock, or when our tale of making a fool of ourselves (again) is met with uncontrollable laughter.

Those reactions feel like a gift. They show that your listener has been engaged and has changed in some way.

You can give the same gift by adding some of these elements.

1. <u>Minimal Encouragers</u>

    When we are genuinely listening, minimal encouragers happen naturally.

    They are the smiles, the "uh huhs", and the nods that show that you are engaged and want the other person to keep going. The official linguistic term is backchanneling.

    But if the stakes are high we can sometimes fall into the trap of only listening for the opportunity to say our bit. We concentrate so hard that we go blank faced and give the impression that the lights are on but nobody's home.

    This is when it is a good idea to do your own internal audit on the quantity and quality of your minimal encouragers.

    - Are you doing them?
    - Are they genuine?

    But beware the danger of looking like a grinning, nodding dog. It's weird.

    Keep those minimal encouragers minimal … and real.

2. <u>The Triple Whammy</u>

The Triple Whammy is a three-part combination move that really shows that you've listened, you've been changed and you want to know more.

It goes like this.

Imagine that someone says to you, "I've just got back from Melbourne and the head of investor relations out there managed to completely turn around the roadshow presentation."

The three moves might go like this.

1. Play back some of their language.

   The experts call this technique "looping".

   You might say, "She managed to turn around the roadshow presentation?" Possibly even with a slight upward inflection of genuine curiosity.

2. Say how that piece of information has changed how you think and/or feel.

   If you get a sense that the speaker is excited about what they have said then allow yourself to match or acknowledge that excitement.[7]

   You might say, "Wow. I didn't think that was even possible given the personalities involved."

3. Ask them to tell you more about it.

   Here the world is your oyster.

> You could use that old favourite: "Can you tell me more about that."
>
> But you could get much more creative with one of the story trigger words.
>
> You might say, "How did she even start to do something like that."
>
> From then on you go back to peeling that onion.

Stories – the API of humanity

I can't emphasise enough how important it is that you allow time and space to co-create the stories that will bring the narrative structure of your DNA of Engagement to life.

Co-creating and sharing stories is the API of humanity.

If you're not familiar with the term API it stands for Application Programming Interface. It's the software that acts as a facilitator to help two very distinct pieces of software work together smoothly.

For example, The Story Spotters recently worked with the CIO of one of the fastest-growing online travel agents in the UK. At the touch of a button his company will give you thousands of complete options for the holiday of your dreams. And all because their APIs let the airlines and hotels talk to each other and come up with solutions that otherwise wouldn't be possible.

Stories help very distinct human beings talk to each other and come up with solutions that otherwise wouldn't be possible.

They are the API of humanity.

The Sarah Jane Adventures

I heard one of the best examples of story as the API of humanity when Amanda Blanc was at a previous organisation and sent her senior leadership team to work with us.

At the start of day one we put each of them in front of the camera and asked them to tell us a story about an experience that had surprised them and changed the way that they thought or felt.

One of those leaders told us about Amanda's first week in charge and the moment when she called him to her office.

As he sat down she said, "I want to know what you are seeing around here. I want to know what you think."

He was amazed. In his whole career he had never been asked this. And certainly not by someone senior who genuinely wanted to hear his answer.

Before this moment he had been on the verge of handing in his resignation. But now he was fully engaged and motivated because Amanda was asking him to be "part of the authorship of the strategy".[8]

Telling your story is great when you need to be understood. But drawing the stories out of others is brilliant when you need to make them *feel* understood.

ENDNOTES

1. Dicks, Matthew *Storyworthy: Engage, Teach, Persuade, and Change Your Life through the Power of Storytelling* (2018) New World Library
2. I won't name him as he uses it to this day.
3. I've toned down her actual reaction to spare the feelings of the innocent.
4. Try this for yourself. It's uncanny how it works.
5. https://www.hgi.org.uk
6. Bowden, Mark. *The Importance of Being Inauthentic* (2013) https://www.youtube.com/watch?v=rk_SMBIW1mg&t=3s (Accessed December 2023)
7. Matching and acknowledgement of mood are central to creating intimacy. Remember the Trust Equation.
8. And we're back to the Howard Schultz quote that opened the book.

SCENE 4: SPREAD YOUR DNA FAR AND WIDE

Day two of a leadership team programme with The Story Spotters always starts with us asking the participants how they've put the ideas into practice.

It's amazing how often we hear, "Well, I haven't really had any opportunities since the last time we saw you."

We always feel like saying, "What? Have you been asleep for a week?"

We are communicating every waking second of our lives. And The DNA of Engagement can help you in many different scenarios.

Here are a few to get you started.

Strategic planning

One of the key areas of our work at The Story Spotters is helping leadership teams put tangible details to their strategic vision.

Our clients often tell us that by helping them to create clarity around the story that they are telling themselves about themselves they quickly reach a point where they can start to implement that story.

Gone are the multiple interpretations and clashing ambitions because everyone can see the DREAM, NIGHTMARES and ACTIONS.

The workshop we've developed feels like a cross between a chat show and a political debate, and one CEO called it the perfect blend of strategic planning, communication skills and team building.

In your Rehearsal Notes think of ways you can use what you've learned to get everyone on the same page with your strategic planning.

Meetings

I recently read a 2023 study from the United States saying that employees waste up to eight hours every week trying to rectify miscommunication.[1] You may be thinking that that figure is way too low.

Another report from 2019 said that over $586bn was being flushed down the drain every year in the USA, UK, Switzerland and Germany alone on poorly organised meetings.[2]

That's the sort of money that would let Elon Musk buy ten Twitters and have plenty of change left over for a decent rebranding exercise.[3]

We believe that these numbers could be slashed by following The DNA of Engagement for Meetings.

A well-structured DNA statement can be shared ahead of time as an agenda. And your DNA is the perfect way to kick off a meeting if you find yourself in the Chair.

1. You will open with the DREAM of what has been agreed so far and what it will mean for the future.

2. You will either state or get consensus on what the potential future NIGHTMARES could be.

3. You will talk about the ACTIONS that will move everything forward.

Of course, as your project progresses and circumstances change, your DNA will change for every meeting. This will be particularly true when you think about the NIGHTMARES and ACTIONS.

You can also use the DNA to help keep the meeting on track if you sense that people are working at cross-purposes.

Gently remind them that:

● We're in the DREAM section here and are brainstorming possibilities.

● We're in the NIGHTMARE section now and are looking for the problems that will get in the way of our dream.

● We're in the ACTION section where we will plan our next steps.

And indeed, you may feel that a meeting should be purely about the DREAM, the NIGHTMARE or the ACTION.

See The DNA of Engagement for Meetings as a short form of Edward de Bono's "Six Thinking Hats".[4]

You'll find a planning sheet in your Rehearsal Notes.

Presentations

Last night I called a friend of mine who had just pre-sented her first paper to her risk committee. When she answered I could hear the noise of a busy bar in the background. Her presentation had either been brilliant or a complete train wreck.

"David, it was amazing," she said. "Brilliant engage-ment. Amazing questions. And they've invited me to give the same presentation to the audit committee next week. But I'm not taking anything for granted. I know that if I don't plan the same way in the future then I could easily slip back into aimless panic."

So, what I'm about to show you is the simple three steps my friend used to ace that risk committee meet-ing and will continue to use from now on. It's called "The DNA of Presenting".

I suspect you can see what I've done there. I've used some narrative transportation and given you a DNA opening for a presentation on how to use The DNA of Engagement. A thoroughly meta state of affairs that might get Christopher Nolan thinking about optioning this book.[5]

Now, I'm sure you've read many books on presentation skills and seen their suggestions on great ways to open a presentation. They usually include things like:

- Ask questions.
- Use a quote.
- Create an interactive activity.
- Pull out a surprising prop.

I want you to add the DNA to that list as it does a number of things that will bring the disparate brains in front of you into parallel thinking.[6]

- It starts with narrative transportation to get everyone imagining the same DREAM.
- It surprises everyone by giving a big but in the NIGHTMARE.
- And it gives certainty by laying out what's to come in the ACTION.

While herding cats is an overused metaphor, it is pretty accurate when it comes to describing the first hurdle you face in any presentation. And with herding complete all you need to do is maintain the engagement.

You can do this in three ways.

1. Make your points with the PRET structure.
2. Use powerful TIRES in your reason.
3. Season your examples with narrative transportation, opinion and metaphor.

In the Rehearsal Notes you'll find a DNA of Engagement sheet for presentations.

Campaigns

Over the years we've spent a lot of our time helping organisations win competitive tenders and individuals win prestigious roles.

Sometimes we have been brought in at the last minute to add some flair to a deadly dull final pitch. But the real magic happens when we become part of the team from kick-off and help build the DNA messaging that will underpin the whole campaign.

When we come in at the end it can feel like putting sticking plasters over holes on the Titanic. But when we're there from the start it feels like building a super yacht.

During any campaign the main thing you are building is trust.

- Can I trust you to deliver on your promise?
- Can I trust you to work well with my people?

And of course, that trust is built on a foundation of understanding.

Remember that line from Theodore Roosevelt that we used earlier? "Nobody cares how much you know until they know how much you care."

Well, a perfect campaign starts with caring for the dreams of those who will select you.

Once you've done that you will have earned the right to show how much you know about the potential nightmares that will get in the way of their dreams, and the actions you will take to overcome those nightmares based on your experience.

At The Story Spotters we've developed a two-day programme for teams who want to put this approach at the heart of their relationship building and business development.

- On day one we look at the DNA skills of telling stories and listening for stories.

- Between sessions we split the group into individual teams and get them to prepare a campaign that is based on a client brief tailored to their industry.

- We set up a scoping call and a coaching call for each team.

- Then on day two we work on delivery skills and move into the final pitches.

Everyone has the opportunity to pitch, be pitched to, and give feedback as outside observers. It's the perfect way to turn the dreams of creating a killer campaign into reality.

You'll find our tools for The DNA of a Killer Pitch in your Rehearsal Notes.

Networking

"So, what do you do?"

It's the question that strikes the fear of God into everyone from the newest joiner to the most seasoned CEO.

But let me tell you a secret. Nobody really cares about what you *do*. They care about the value you deliver.

And guess what? We've got a DNA worksheet that helps you craft your answer to that killer question.

We were going to call it the DNA Elevator Pitch. But we haven't ... because we hate it.

You'll find The DNA Champagne Spiel in your Rehearsal Notes.

It's guaranteed to make your listener forget that glass of bubbling Moët and ask you to tell them more.

Interviews

A lot of interviews these days are strengths based and the expectation is that you will be able to clearly articulate the value you will bring to the role that you are applying for.

The DNA of Engagement works perfectly when you get the question, "Tell me about a time when you..."

All you need to do is plan in this way.

1. Identify a situation in your life when you had to show a similar set of strengths to those that your new role requires.
2. Use the PRET message structure.
3. Bring the example to life using narrative transportation and a DNA structure.

We've used this approach with people going for partnership roles in the Big 4 and people being grilled for senior positions in the FTSE100.

One time when it worked very well was with a client who knew that the role she was applying for needed a mixture of resilience and innovative thinking.

Her PRET answer to "tell me a bit about yourself" looked like this.

- Point – Well a lot of my friends and family say that I am like an inquisitive terrier. I'm fascinated by finding new solutions to old problems and then I won't let go until I've got it done.
- Reason – Which from everything I've read about the way you work here seems really important.
- Example – For example ... and then she went on to tell a quick and vivid story about how she had single-handedly renovated a derelict house by watching YouTube videos and overcoming a mountain of challenges.[7]

> ● Takeaway – She reiterated the key points of resilience and innovation that she wanted the panel to remember.

I spoke to her after she had been appointed to the role and she said that the panel had spent very little time talking about the job itself. Everyone had been so fascinated in plumbing and plastering.

You'll find The DNA of Strengths Stories in your Rehearsal Notes.

Life in general

The Sarah Jane Adventures

> The thing I love about The DNA of Engagement is that it works everywhere.
>
> You can use it in so many work situations. But it stands up really well to the toughest domestic challenges.
>
> One of my favourite pieces of feedback came after a workshop we delivered to a DE&I team. It went like this.
>
> "Your model has helped me a lot. I've really understood how I can influence the business leaders to

take more proactive steps to embed diversity and inclusion. But it really came into its own this weekend while I was wedding planning with my fiancé!"

Now that's really putting the DNA to the test.

Try it on your partner, your toddler or your teenager, and let me know how you get on.

ENDNOTES

1. communicate4IMPACT Businesses Can Finally Quantify the Costs of Poor Communication 2023 (Accessed April 2024) https://www.communicate4impact.com/blog/the-costs-of-poor-communication

2. BOOQED *Minutes (Wasted) of Meeting: 50 Shocking Meeting Statistics* 2023 (Accessed January 2024) https://www.booqed.com/blog/minutes-wasted-of-meeting-50-shocking-meeting-statistics

3. Elon ... X ... really?

4. de Bono, Edward *Six Thinking Hats: The multi-million bestselling guide to running better meetings and making faster decisions* (2016) Penguin Life

5. Please tread softly on my dreams.

6. Parallel thinking is the process of getting a group to think the same way.

7. If you are creating one of these strengths-based stories then don't forget to add the nightmares you had to overcome. Strengths are only strengths because they have been put to the test.

ACT THREE

SCENE 1: THE ONLY WAY IS ETHICS

The techniques you have been learning and practising are incredibly powerful. You only need to take a quick glance over recent history to see that.

Narrative control and storytelling have been used to build trust, drive engagement and influence change in so many areas of our lives.

But in the words of the proverb popularised by Spiderman, "With great power comes great responsibility." You can use The DNA of Engagement for good or you can use it for ill.

As a result, I implore every one of you to do an ethics audit on your messaging. If you are going to build trust and influence change, do it from the right place.

One of my favourite people in the story community is the American David Hutchens.

David is not only a master story craftsman who has worked with organisations such as L'Oreal, NASA and Coca-Cola, but he has a heart the size of the Appalachian Mountains that lie on his doorstep.

A few months ago, he published what he calls his Story Manifesto. It is a list of conditions that he feels are necessary if you want to call yourself a story professional.[1]

Here are some that really stood out for me.

- Commit to truth in your stories.
- Cherish the deep humanity of others.
- Reveal your own humanity.
- Invite the stories of those you don't agree with.
- Recognise that meaning is not built into the story but is communally negotiated.
- Accept that your interpretation of the story is only the beginning of a conversation; it's never the last word.
- Respect the great power that stories hold ... as well as the great harm they can cause.
- Know that asking for stories is a higher calling than telling them.
- Be willing to be changed by another's story.

Sound familiar?

It won't surprise you that The Story Spotters stand wholeheartedly behind everything David says.

But there is another test you can put your messaging through if you really want to establish its ethical rigour.

The TARES Test

In 2001 Sherry Baker and David L. Martinson developed what they call The TARES Test – the five principles of ethical persuasion.

TARES stands for Truthfulness, Authenticity, Respect, Equity and Social Responsibility.[2]

Here are some questions you can ask yourself about your message before you put The DNA of Engagement into action.

Truthfulness

- Have I left out any important information?
- If so, did I do it deliberately in order to misdirect the other party?
- Would I feel the message was complete if I heard it?

Authenticity

- Do I truly believe in what I am saying?
- Do I feel good about delivering this message?
- Does my message make others believe things that I don't?
- Do I believe the recipient of this message will benefit?

Respect

- Does my message allow space for the recipient to come to their own conclusions?
- Will my message benefit the recipient?

- Does my message respect their rights and well-being?
- Does my message just serve me or my aims?

Equity

- Would I think my message was fair if I heard it?
- Would I feel happy for those I love and care about to hear this message?
- Do the people hearing my message know that they play a role in the outcome and are not just being "told what to do"?
- Am I exploiting an imbalance of power?

Social responsibility

- Will the successful outcome of my appeal create a world that I would be happy for my nearest and dearest to live in?
- Does my message help build public trust?
- Does my message create space for debate?
- Have I fairly represented the ideas and behaviours of all the parties I have spoken about?

Consider your answers to all these questions and do an ethics audit on your messaging. Then prepare to take The DNA of Engagement Oath.

The DNA of Engagement Oath

I want you to go and get a copy of your chosen religious text, your favourite album or your most loved cookbook. I'll be here when you come back.

Now, I want you to place your left hand on that text, album or cookbook and raise your right hand.

Repeat after me:

I (insert your name here) do hereby acknowledge that The DNA of Engagement holds mighty powers.

Those powers will enable me to build trust, drive engagement and influence change from this day on.

I also acknowledge that with these powers come great responsibility. The responsibility to create changes that are good as opposed to evil.

Evil changes range from (but are not confined to)

- *Influencing my partner to eat in restaurants that I know they will actively dislike.*
- *Aiding and abetting the election of political nut jobs.*

With this in mind, I do solemnly swear that I will only undertake acts of change that could be considered beneficial to all.

However, if I do choose to act with malevolent intent, all liability will rest solely with myself.

Neither David Pullan, Sarah Jane McKechnie, nor any current or future representative of The Story Spotters shall be held responsible.

This I swear in the name of (Insert name of deity, rock god or celebrity chef as appropriate).

Signed

....

Please take 5 minutes to leave us a review, it helps other people to decide if they want to read the book, and we'll be eternally grateful. If you're reading on Kindle just scroll to the end of the book. If you're reading the paperback, please go to your favourite bookstore.

Remember, you can get the promised downloads at www.TheDNAofEngagement.com or scan the QR code.

ENDNOTES

1. Hutchens, David *The David Hutchens Story Manifesto* (Accessed January 2024) https://www.linkedin.com/feed/update/urn:li:activity:7125454502458994691?updateEntityUrn=urn%3Ali%3Afs_feedUpdate%3A%28V2%2Curn%3Ali%3Aactivity%3A7125454502458994691%29

2. Sherry Baker & David L. Martinson (2001) The TARES Test: Five Principles for Ethical Persuasion, Journal of Mass Media Ethics, 16:2-3, 148-175, DOI: 10.1080/08900523.2001.9679610

3. World Economic Forum *Trudeau: The pace of change has never been this fast* 2018 https://youtu.be/fTI1YNTNb0g?si=fUW0eavk7Fb8hcQU (Accessed March 2024)

SCENE 2: ARE YOU READY FOR THIS?

At Davos in 2018 the Canadian Prime Minister Justin Trudeau said, "The pace of change has never been this fast, yet it will never be this slow again."[3]

The years since then seem to have proved him right.

While specific concerns might vary from industry to industry, the changes in digital transformation, cybersecurity, workforce dynamics, the climate, sustainability and geopolitics just keep on coming.

We wrote this book because we believe that the leaders who steer a successful course through these changes will be the leaders who can create the space and time to bring people together to be part of the solution.

We hope that you share this belief and agree with the following principles.

1. Change isn't done *to* people; it's done *with* people.

2. The ideas behind that change need a strong narrative structure that is based on mutual understanding.

3. Once you've achieved that understanding it's cru-cial that you help others co-create the stories that will support the narrative.

We believe that The DNA of Engagement is the tool to help you achieve these things.

It will give you the skills to build trusted relationships and create the space and time to stay ahead of the pace.

You *have* to be ready for this.

The IP of the DNA

There is one thing we need to make clear about what you have read in this book. We claim no intellectual property rights over any of it.

We might hold trademarks over The DNA of Engagement® and The Story Spotters® but if anyone tells you that they own IP over story work you might like to remind them that if Aristotle ever gets a lawyer then they are really in trouble.

At best we claim an intellectual perspective, which is based on many years of putting story-based techniques to the test as we've supported leaders and their teams around the globe.

But the real IP of the DNA involves two things.

1. Information – the reason why things work and how they work.
2. Practical Tools – the things you can use immediately to build trust, drive engagement and influence change.

Here is a reminder of all the Information (I) and Practical Tools (P) we've covered.

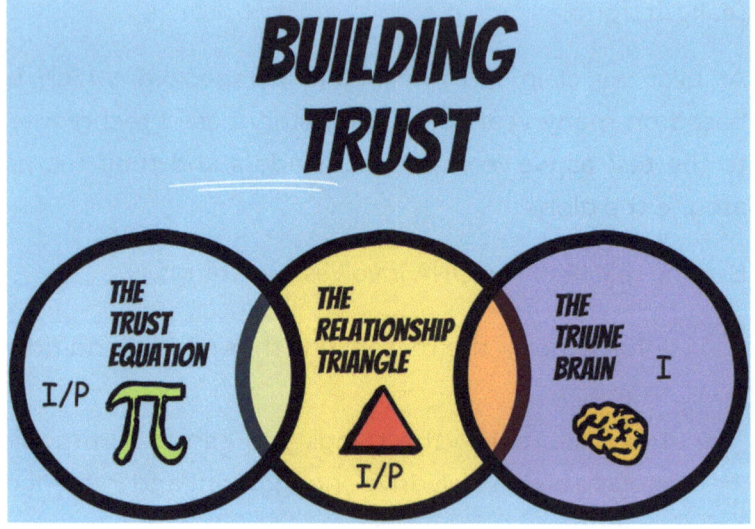

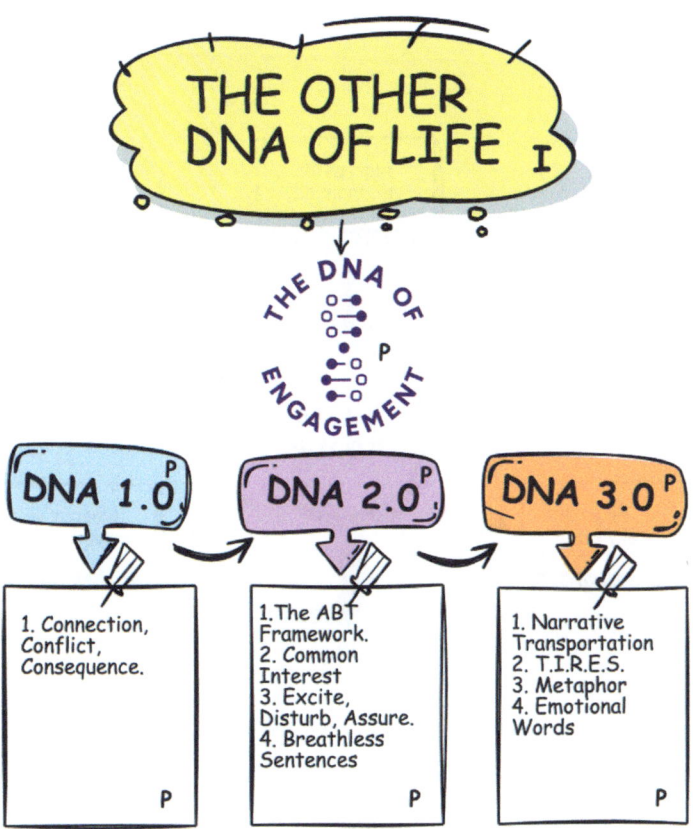

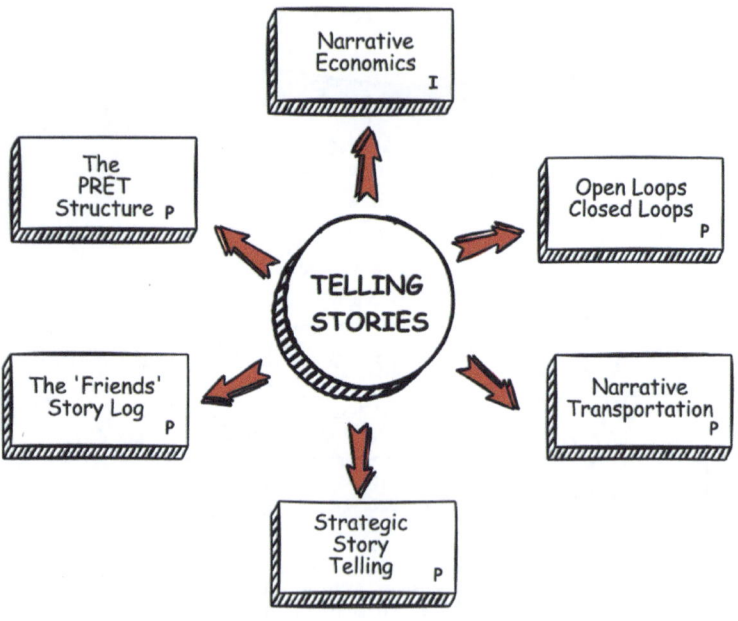

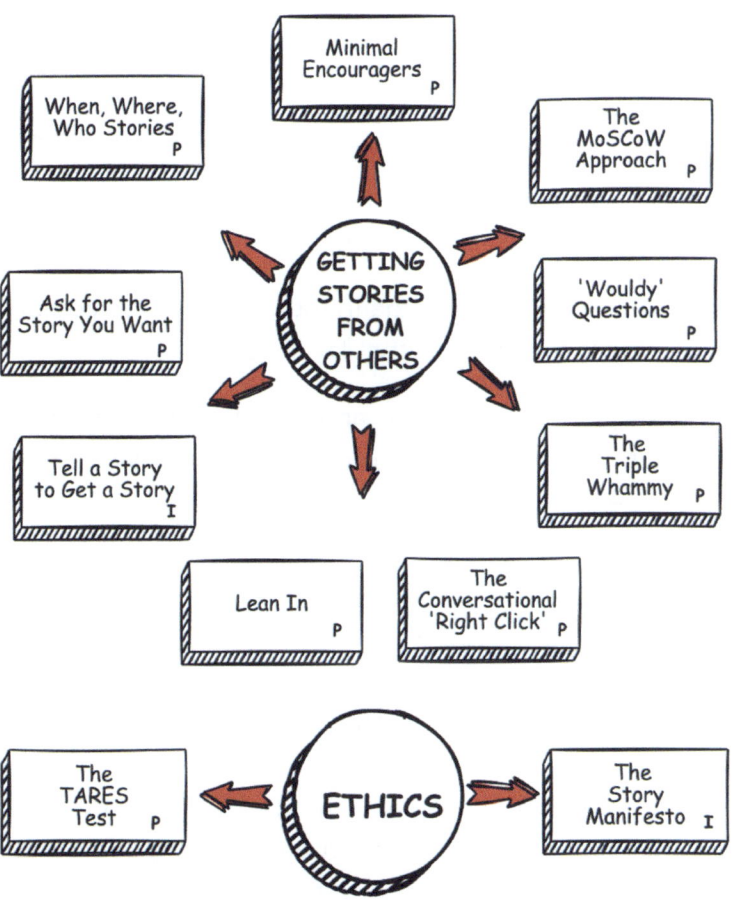

Use them well and please keep in touch. We'd love to know how you get on.

ROLL CREDITS

There's one person that we both have to thank for this book. And that person is Ken Blanc.

Ken, when you put Amanda in touch with us we couldn't have imagined the years that lay ahead.

Amanda, working with you and your leaders has been a true gift. We've learned as much from them as we hope they have from us.

Danny Harmer and Renarta Guy, your support as we developed and tested The DNA of Engagement throughout 2023 was extraordinary.

Thank you also to the wonderful Debs Jenkins from https://shortvaluablebooks.com/ Your combination of process, artistry and humour is something every author should experience. And you create amazing writing cohorts full of laughter, wisdom and support. Anne Walsh and Sharon Eden, Monday at 3 p.m. GMT will never be quite the same.

Louise Bonham, we wrote this book with you in mind. Our sole aim was to produce something that you would find valuable and enjoyable. Your feedback was the quantum leap we needed, and if we haven't put it into action then you know where we live.

Massive thanks also to our story sources. Brian Spinks, Georgina Smith, Tina Higgins, Angela Brav, Henry Daubeney, Jono Gill – your words take up very special places on The Story Spotter "hard drive".

Every book needs a super squad of beta readers and we lucked out by getting one that combined both subject matter experts and great writers. Sara Rajeswaran, Troy Andrews, Kiran Francis, Aman Hayer, Charlotte Otter, Owen McFeeley, Alex English, Clare Best, Andrew Potter and Helen Ingram, your insight and refinements have been invaluable.

David Gifford from https://www.inscriptdesign.com/ your illustrations were the final lift our book needed. And Abhay Chettri, your video editing wizardry has added huge value to the Rehearsal Notes.

And last but not least, Charlie Pullan. You are one of the best storytellers we know. Every day as your parents is a day well spent.

LET'S HAVE COFFEE

We hope you've enjoyed this book and found it both enjoyable and useful. All you have to do now is put it into action.

One of our clients recently compared The DNA of Engagement to Agile.

He said, "It's easy to understand and difficult to master ... but not impossible."

If you want to talk to us about how we can help you master The DNA of Engagement and apply it in your business, do get in touch.

We love nothing more than using a combination of coaching, consulting and training to help you connect to the hearts and minds of your stakeholders.

Here are some ideas for you to think about.

- We run programmes to help individual leaders and teams use The DNA.
- We help business development teams embed The DNA in their organisations.
- We facilitate DNA conversations that clarify the strategic narrative.

- We coach individuals to use The DNA in big job interviews and key presentations.

- We add the spark to events with keynotes on The DNA.

- We mentor pitch teams on how The DNA will help them win competitive tenders.

Basically, if you'd love to raise your DNA game we'd love to talk.

Please feel free to look at our website www.thestoryspot-ters.com or get in touch at hello@thestoryspotters.com

SOME BOOKS YOU'LL LOVE

The Heart of Business by Hubert Joly tells the story of how the former CEO of Best Buy increased customer satisfaction, grew the stock price and made his company a leader in innovation and sustainability … by putting people and purpose first.

The Disconnect Principle: Eliminate Difficult Conversations with Clarity and Empathy by Ann Latham feels like the sister book to this one. Her insight into the power of doing things "with others" rather than "to others" is brilliant.

Connect by Simon Lancaster reveals his communication secrets on how to connect with people's deepest instincts and emotions. Come armed with a marker pen. This one is crammed with practical tips.

Bridges and Barriers by Troy Andrews is a great guide to behavioural science and helps you understand how and why people make decisions and judgements.

Circle of the 9 Muses by David Hutchens captures the best practices of the world's most influential story consultants. It's like an Aladdin's Cave of story work.

The Narrative Gym for Business by Randy Olson and Park Howell will give you some fantastic insight into the ABT Framework.

Storyworthy by Matthew Dicks shows you how to tell a great story – and why doing so matters. He's a five-time Moth GrandSLAM winner, so he knows a thing or two.

ABOUT US

Hello. It's Sarah Jane again.

This really is the last word. I've sent David to the shops.

One Monday morning many years ago, the two of us walked into a rehearsal room and decided that we'd met the person who was going to get us through the six-month tour that lay ahead.

I don't think either of us expected the extraordinary journey that we've been on since then.

- We've acted in films with Shirley MacLaine and performed to Henry Kissinger and his Secret Service entourage.

- We've created storytelling shows where we've cooked chicken for the audience.
- We've developed an improvisation course called "Don't Be Hostage to the Funny."

And now, we apply the science, art and craft of story to the communications challenges that our clients face in industries such as professional and financial services, engineering, pharmaceutical, retail, hospitality, tech and the public sector.

I made the first leap into the world of business storytelling after our son was born. And David joined me a couple of years later.

I remember him calling me from the foyer of a skyscraper in Canary Wharf before one of his first solo gigs and saying, "Sarah Jane, I'm not like these people."

I said to him, "And that's exactly why you're there. They know *what* they do. But you know how to help them spot and share the stories that will make sense of it."

He listened. And together we've racked up over forty combined years helping leaders and their teams connect to customers and colleagues at the moments that matter.

No two days have been the same and it's been a lot of what we call "serious fun".

I could go on but I expect you've got other things to do.

If you want to have a chat about how our work can be applied to your organisational or personal goals then please do email us on hello@thestoryspotters.com. We'd love to share some stories with you.

Which brings me to my favourite closing line of all time.

"Fly, my pretties. Fly!"[1]

ENDNOTES

1.   Our editor Lisa de Caux was deeply concerned that we were ending the book by misquoting the Wicked Witch in *The Wizard of Oz*. If, like Lisa, you are an aficionado of that great film I want to reassure you of one thing. We are actually correctly quoting Mr Burns from The Simpsons Season 5 Episode 9 *The Last Temptation of Homer*. You're welcome.

MORE PRAISE FOR THE DNA OF ENGAGEMENT

DNA: Do Not Avoid this masterful book! You'll read it, return to it, and rely on it every time you need to influence minds and create lasting change.

Leanne Hughes, author of The 2-Hour Workshop Blueprint and host of the First Time Facilitator podcast

Dogs sniff each other, monkeys groom each other, humans tell stories. Read this book and learn how to be an effective human.

Andrew Ratcliffe – non-executive director Barclays Bank UK PLC, Chair of Audit & Risk Assurance Committee Royal College of Music, Board of Trustees University of London

Brilliant advice that I'm planning to pretend I thought of first.

Stuart Goldsmith – Climate Comedy Supercharger and host of The Comedian's Comedian Podcast

Shhh... This is the book you won't want your competitors to find out about!

Jane Montgomery – International Sales Manager turned Psychology Geek

David and Sarah Jane reveal their secrets with heart, intelligence, and wit. I've been in the corporate communication game for three decades and I learned a lot from The DNA of Engagement.

David Hutchens – www.TheStoryTellingLeader.com

Any leader looking to shape strategic perceptions and inspire action will find a highly original approach that gets everyone speaking the same language of change.

Henry Daubeney – Non-Executive Director OSB Group PLC

Short, punchy, fun and full of golden nuggets. Read it quickly. Study it purposefully. And prepare to benefit from more rewarding and effective interactions.

Andrew Potter - Executive Coach, Former CEO NCP Ltd and Strategic Advisor to the UN World Food Programme

A fabulous read full of fun anecdotes and strong helpful information to inspire and effect change. I will take it into my daily leadership style.

Bronwyn Camac – Director, Geological Survey of South Australia, Department for Energy and Mining

For those of us kicking off our journey, this book is like wielding a megaphone that ensures our voices are heard and have the power to drive change from the get-go!

Suzy Parish – Quantum Data Community & Partnerships Manager Aviva

Compelling, concise and lively. This is a first-class weaving together of science, experience, wisdom and intuition, that shows why and how stories matter in every area of our lives.

Clare Best – poet, memoirist, Lecturer in Creative Writing

The DNA of Engagement is more than just must-read. It is a Swiss Army Story toolkit that supercharges communication in business and in life.

Mark Murray – IT Director Frontier Economics

I had the thought over and over - if I could hold onto this during key moments at work, it would change everything.

Greg Detre – Rogue AI Engineer, cofounder of Memrise and former Chief Data Scientist of Channel 4

The beauty of this book is that you can pick it up over and over again. And I have. When you feel like it's hard to connect with people the DNA will help you no end.

John Dillon – Partner PwC International and Domestic Business Leader

I'm certain that all change is built on human connections. And we forge those connections with stories that build trust. If this is what you need, you need to read this book.

Hortense Frisby - Chief of Staff, Executive Coach & Founder of Coaching with Chemistry

It's so rare that a business book engages you completely from start to finish. I was nodding, smiling and applying David and Sarah Jane's thinking to current problems I'm trying to solve.

Georgina Smith - Divisional Director Standard Bank Group

David and Sarah Jane's DNA approach has helped us craft the storytelling around our mission to re-imagine medicine, so we improve and extend people's lives.

Reinhard Moschitz - Executive Director, Customer & Content Strategy, Novartis Pharmaceuticals, Switzerland

The DNA of Engagement encapsulates what I have experienced to be key to achieving happiness and living life with purpose, both at work and beyond.

Philippe Guijarro, UK Life Insurance Leader and Wellbeing and mental health leader for PwC in Scotland

Concise, well-written and it gets great results. I know. Like so many business leaders I respect I've experienced the David and Sarah Jane approach.

Thomas Hull – Chair of Audit and Risk Committee Zurich Reinsurance

This is a book I will keep going back to for inspiration.

Owen McFeely - Director Advisory Services, Retail & Consumer Practice, PwC Ireland

What a delightful mixture of stories and solid research. I came for the movies and stayed for the data. Now I'm off to make someone a DNA offer they can't refuse.

Anne Walsh – The Excel Lady

In a world of distraction The DNA of Engagement is a fantastic guide for anyone who needs to deliver an unmistakable message with maximum impact.

Catherine Lang-Cline – CEO & host of 'The Secret Art of Business®'

Story, insight and actionable stuff. I was gripped and intrigued from the beginning and can see myself dipping into this work of GOLD for a long time to come.

Katie Skelton – Business owner and fan of words

This book could be the Bible for investor engagement. I'm embarking on a new pitch and the DNA has helped me to spot the gaps I need to close before I hit launch!

Jess Flack - Digital Inclusion Lead Officer, Essex County Council

Rugby players, sharks and celery seeds all feature in David and Sarah Jane's stories about how to deepen connections and create influence. It's fun, it's informative and I'll be recommending it to my clients.

Mica Allan – The Communication Skills Wizard ™

As a consultant whose clients are aiming to ethically influence massive societal changes, this fabulous book has inspired me to use the DNA framework as a strategic tool for building trust and connection. It's a gamechanger.

Katrina Fox – Storytelling Consultant

This is a wonderful book about the heart and head of business. I love how David and Sarah Jane understand that trust is the essential scaffolding of being able to work together.

Patrice Sullivan – Couple and Individual Psychotherapist, Tavistock Relationships

Entertaining. Engaging. Challenging. Grab a notepad and prepare to enjoy it as much I did.

Danny Denhard - Coach, consultant, advisor

If the DNA of Engagement doesn't knock your socks off, nothing will. It's for all areas of your life, including moody teenagers if you have them. I couldn't put it down!

Sharon Eden - The Wild Elder and author of "RE-DISCOVERED – Down & Dirty Spirituality to revitalise who you really are, where you're going and what you came here to do"

Witty and fun, just like the authors, The DNA of Engagement gives teams, leaders and individual contributors all the tools they need to engage others on the journey of change.

Charlotte Otter – Communicator and Writer

I closed the book with a sigh of satisfaction, knowing I'd come away from the reading with stronger skills in my story toolkit.

Sally Murphy – Founder of Welltold

I urge you to read The DNA of Engagement and pick up the 'secret sauce' from people who know their stuff. It will help deliver a better you and a better business.

Lawrie Philpott – CEO Philpott Black

This book is a total gem. I'll be dipping into it every time I need to nail a pitch.

Alex English – Author and screenwriter

In just two hours with The DNA of Engagement, I picked up more storytelling tricks than I ever did from all my other books combined—and trust me, I've got a library card! This book is like a turbo-charged espresso shot for your narrative skills.

Debbie Jenkins – Author & Publisher

BV - #0018 - 070325 - C0 - 203/127/10 - PB - 9781908770677 - Matt Lamination